Animated

 Earth

Animated
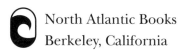
Earth

A Story of
Peruvian Whistles
and Transformation

SECOND EDITION

Daniel K. Statnekov

North Atlantic Books
Berkeley, California

Published by
North Atlantic Books   Cover photos: Vicus vessel by Mara
P.O. Box 12327   Statnekov; Machu Picchu by Ed Chapell
Berkeley, California 94712   Cover and book design by Paula Morrison

Printed in the United States of America

Animated Earth is sponsored by the Society for the Study of Native Arts and Sciences, a nonprofit educational corporation whose goals are to develop an educational and crosscultural perspective linking various scientific, social, and artistic fields; to nurture a holistic view of arts, sciences, humanities, and healing; and to publish and distribute literature on the relationship of mind, body, and nature.

North Atlantic Books' publications are available through most bookstores. For further information, call 800-337-2665 or visit our website at www.northatlanticbooks.com.

Substantial discounts on bulk quantities are available to corporations, professional associations, and other organizations. For details and discount information, contact our special sales department.

Library of Congress Cataloging-in-Publication Data
Statnekov, Daniel K., 1943–
    Animated earth : a story of Peruvian whistles and transformation / by Daniel K. Statnekov.– 2nd ed.
        p. cm.
Includes bibliographical references and index.
    ISBN 1-55643-463-4 (pbk.)
    1. Vases, Acoustic—Miscellanea.   2. Chimu pottery.   3. Indian pottery—Peru.   4. Statnekov, Daniel K., 1943–   I. Title.
    BF1999.S719 2003
    001.94–dc21

                                    2003010694

1   2   3   4   5   6   7   8   9   DATA   08   07   06   05   04   03

For Mara, Jacob, and Isaac,
and those who will follow

Acknowledgments

I have been sustained in my life and in my work by great love. My parents and my grandparents, my uncles and aunts, my brother and sisters, my cousins, and my wives and children: all have bestowed upon me the great treasure of my life. Friends have also loved me into being. I've thought about listing them here, but each and every one of them is too precious for me to include on a list. Those of you who read this already know you are my loved ones. All of you have given me sustenance throughout this journey, and all of you are indelibly imbued in my heart.

I thank Richard Grossinger for his support in publishing the second edition of this book. Special thanks are due to Sarah Serafimidis, my project editor at North Atlantic Books, who suggested that my struggle to grow into a whole person was as important a theme as was the whistles' discovery. I am grateful for Sarah's perspective, which encouraged me to reflect upon and recount my personal journey in a deeper way in this book. Laura Derocher lovingly taught me the finer points of writing as she edited and helped me revise the original manuscript. Due to Laura's insistence, I included a number of synchronicities that occurred at key junctures in my story, to underscore how Spirit is at play in our lives. Pam Suwinsky provided the final edit. Thank you, Pam for adding luster to my words and clarity to my writing. I also thank Paula Morrison for creating the cover for this second edition and for helping to produce a truly beautiful book.

Finally, I am thankful to that force within the Creation that has enabled me to experience love through my being.

Prologue

IN 1949, A BRITISH SCHOLAR, Adrian Digby, flew from London to New York to present a paper to the 29th Session of the International Congress of Americanists. Digby's paper, entitled "The Technical Development of Whistling Vases in Peru," offered an explanation for the invention of a peculiar type of whistling ceramic vessel made by various archaic Andean cultures. The British scholar's conclusion, that the pots were made to whistle because of a Peruvian potter's "happy accident," was duly noted in the proceedings of the Congress, and subsequently—as is often the case in such matters—became the generally accepted academic interpretation.

After a time of decay comes the turning point.

—*I Ching*

Y EARS EARLIER, WHEN I WAS A BOY, someone told me the story
of Vishnu the Hindu god who, upon blowing into a conch
shell, destroyed the world. It was just a story then, a folktale from
India. No more real than *Alice in Wonderland* or the story of Aladdin
and his lamp. But that was before I bought the curious old vase.

I remember the night I found it. Winter was not quite over,
and the cold rain that fell that evening would have iced the roads
had the temperature dropped by a few degrees. The drizzle had
already begun when I set out from my home in Chester County,
Pennsylvania, to attend an auction in nearby Delaware County. I
was driving a gold Cadillac at the time, a four-door Sedan de Ville
that had been a gift from my wife's grandmother, Mrs. Townsend.
I enjoyed that car. It fit my self-image as an affluent country squire,
entrepreneur, and collector of antiques. I felt secure driving the
luxury automobile past the neat farms, orchards, and country
estates that proliferate in the distant suburb of Philadelphia known
in society as home for the "horsy set."

Chester County is an historical area, site of the Revolutionary
War, Battle of the Brandywine. My wife, Barbara Townsend Mans-

field, could trace her ancestry to before the American Revolution, in fact to the Mayflower landing. We lived in a gracious stone colonial home built in the eighteenth century by a friend of Benjamin Franklin. Attached to the house was a kennel for Barbara's Italian Greyhounds, and our property included a barn and carriage shed, along with an orchard, gardens, and a well-tended lawn. The Brandywine River meandered through our little estate, and living "on the Brandywine" was a mark of prestige in the community.

As I drove toward the auction, I passed Andrew Wyeth's home in historic Chadds Ford, and Lafayette's headquarters on the edge of the battlefield. I also passed the Chadds Ford Inn, a tavern I had frequented when I was still single, hoping to meet young women from the surrounding affluent community. The Cadillac moved through the rain like a silent tank, and I fantasized about what new treasure I might discover at the sale. Perhaps an early Windsor chair or a spatterware teacup to join the collection of old American china displayed in our corner cupboard. Nearly every furnishing in our home had been fashioned in colonial times. Barbara's friends, many of them members of socially prominent families, had remarked on the quality of our antiques. Most of my childhood friends wouldn't know a Chippendale from an Airedale, and that was part of the reason I had married Barbara in the first place.

The near-freezing rain held the promise of a light turnout at the auction. If there were anything worthwhile at the sale it would probably be a bargain. Only a devoted collector or a very hungry dealer would brave this miserable weather to drive to an old auction barn stuck in the middle of nowhere. I loved searching for antiques and took pleasure in knowing that if I really wanted something, more often than not, I could buy it. The previous year I had finally sold my grandfather's machine shop. For five years I had driven more than an hour each way to work in the run-down

Germantown section of Philadelphia. Now I was free of its dreariness and, in a very real sense, I was benefiting from my grandfather's success.

Louis Kassvan, my maternal grandfather, had emigrated from Romania at the turn of the century and had built several businesses, the last of which was a precision machine shop located in Philadelphia. Grandpapa had died within six months of my going to work for him. Without a technical understanding of the machining process, I ended up working in administration and sales. The buyers for the companies with which we did business barely hid their contempt for the grandson who had inherited an easy job in a business he knew nothing about. I was too new in the company to have earned the respect of the employees either. When the opportunity came to sell the business, I jumped at it. My share of the proceeds had provided me with a nucleus of capital to invest; combined with Barbara's inheritance, we were affluent.

Ethnic or tribal art did not interest me, so I was surprised, shortly after arriving at the auction, to find myself drawn to a black earthenware vase of curious form and unknown provenance. The artifact was comprised of two connected chambers. One chamber was modeled in the form of a seated figure with his hands clasped in front of him, while the other resembled a bottle with a spout. The figure wore nothing distinctive to identify him or to signify his station in life, but his whole expression conveyed to me a deep sense of peace or equanimity. Instinctively, I surmised the vessel had been made in ancient times, probably by an Indian from some tribe in South America. It looked to me as if the artifact had been constructed as a whistle.

Out of curiosity, I blew into the spout for a moment. The sound was surprisingly loud, and several people who were previewing the auction turned toward me. Self-conscious, I stopped blowing into the bottle and made a gesture to imply my amusement with the artifact as well. But something had already happened. Instantly, and beyond all reason, my fervent desire was to own the whistling pot. I had previously suffered the collector's affliction of having to possess something or other, but nothing compared to my yearning for the ancient relic. I had to have it.

Unlike anything else in my experience, the sound of the whistling bottle beckoned with a special intimation. It was nothing I could specifically identify, but whatever it was reached out across the centuries of dust and forgetfulness to stir ever so slightly a forgotten promise, as if a faint breeze had touched a part of me of which I had been unaware.

My wife had been out in the rain that evening as well. After an earlier appointment with her seamstress, Barbara had driven to the auction with a friend. As the two attractive women in their early thirties made their way toward me through the sparse crowd, I noticed the appreciative looks given to them by some of the other men. Barbara was a classic beauty: blond, blue-eyed, with the bearing that would identify her in any social situation as a woman of the upper class. Despite the difference in our backgrounds, we had been attracted to each other from our first meeting. Barbara had two children to raise from her previous marriage, and my willingness to become their stepfather closed the gap that might have otherwise remained after exploring our initial attraction. For me, Barbara represented an entrée into the social world to which I aspired. We married less than a month after we met. Even though my wife shared my enthusiasm for collecting antiques, she looked slightly askance when I showed her the old clay whistle that so excited me.

I tried as best I could to explain what I myself did not understand. "There's something about this old vase," I told her. "I feel as if I've seen it before.... Somehow it seems familiar, but I don't think I've ever seen anything like it. Maybe I saw a picture of something like it somewhere, but that still wouldn't explain this feeling I have about it. I know it doesn't fit in with anything else we've collected, but it's important to me. I'm going to buy it!"

Barbara agreed that the old black vase was quite unlike our spatterware and other early china collections, but if I felt that strongly about it she had no objection to my acquiring it.

It was late in the evening, close to midnight, when the vessel was finally put up for sale, and then only upon my insistence was it offered at all. Apparently the auctioneer was holding the piece back, along with several others, perhaps to sell them more advantageously at another time. After a lull in the bidding, the man wielding the gavel asked, "Is there anything else before we call it a night?"

"Yes," I cried out loudly, surprised at the intensity in my voice. "That piece over there in the glass case. I've been waiting for it all night." My tone of voice was demanding, holding the promise of an argument, and the auctioneer—seemingly directed by my urgency—retrieved the item I had indicated.

Holding it up, he looked at it and then humorously remarked, "A genuine article right out of King Tut's tomb. What am I bid?"

No one said anything for a few seconds, and then someone called out, "Five dollars!" I joined in the bidding and, in what seemed only a few seconds, I had purchased the pottery artifact for thirty dollars. Returning home with my acquisition, I carefully tucked it away in my study to await the completion of a more pressing endeavor.

At the time, my main interest, aside from collecting antiques and living the life of a country gentleman, was a speech I was preparing to give at the annual stockholders' meeting of the Foote Mineral Company. Headquartered in nearby Downingtown, Pennsylvania, Foote Mineral was an international mining company with worldwide business interests. I first became aware of the company because of articles in the local newspaper reporting that students from a nearby black college were picketing the corporate offices. My interest piqued, I studied the issues involved. My college degree was in international relations, and though my business experience was limited, I was able to read a financial statement. I concluded that Foote Mineral was ripe for a takeover.

The company was losing money at a furious rate. Its management had also been accused of exploitative labor practices and de facto support of a white supremacist political regime in Rhodesia, where Foote Mineral owned and operated chromium mines. Since selling my grandfather's machine shop, I had been looking for something substantial to do in the business community, some situation where I could be the originator and take credit for an accomplishment. I decided this was my opportunity. I became a stockholder with the intent of organizing an opposition to take control of the company.

I hoped to win the support of the other stockholders by formulating a constructive plan to make the company profitable again. I intended to turn the social issues to my advantage as well. The chromium mines were not profitable, unnecessary to the financial reorganization I envisioned, and Foote Mineral could well afford to turn them over to the black Africans as a symbol of American corporate responsibility. I might not have been able to do this legally, but I fantasized that the announcement of my intentions to return assets to a politically oppressed people would propel me into the limelight as an important, socially conscious young businessman. I also entertained the idea that this might be the beginning of a high-profile political career for me as well.

The annual meeting of stockholders was scheduled for the end of April, and I occupied much of my time preparing to present my plan. I would walk around my property, memorizing from typewritten cards both a speech I hoped would convince the other stockholders to vote for an alternative slate of directors that I intended to nominate, and my business plan to reorganize the firm. If I could just convince the major stockholders at the meeting, I thought, the momentum of my success would delineate my future. Not only would I have the trappings of success, I would gain the measure of it as well.

It was about a month after the auction, on the day after the Foote Mineral meeting, when I turned my attention once again to the ancient relic. Undoubtedly, the outcome of my effort with regard to the mining company played a pivotal role in what was about to occur. My speech had been well received, and a reporter for the *Wall Street Journal* had interviewed me, but I had failed to elect even a single director to the company's board. I had been counting on being successful. Almost without realizing it, I had been staking my future on it. Now my dream, along with the color copies of my business plan, lay abandoned on the floor and empty seats in the room where the corporate meeting had taken place. The following morning ushered in a harsh dawn. I was faced with the unavoidable question: What was I *really* doing with my life?

Looking back, I had very few childhood memories. The years seemed to blur together, punctuated by changing schools or moving to a new house or another city. My grammar school adventures consisted of exploring the woods behind our house, stalking bullfrogs and birds with a homemade spear, and imagining myself a woodsman like Davy Crockett as portrayed by Disney.

My most memorable experience was being hit by a car in the fifth grade and suffering a broken leg. I was out of school for nearly a year, and although I was promoted to the sixth grade (having been tutored at home), I was never able to participate fully in sports afterward. When I was in the seventh grade my family moved to California. In Los Angeles I felt like a duck out of water. Being an "easterner" and not able to keep up with the other fellows on the playing field, I made very few friends. Three years later we moved back to Delaware, and I found that the intervening years had severed my grammar school friendships.

In the eleventh grade I transferred to Wilmington Friends School, a private school founded by Quakers. For the most part, my classmates at Friends were from affluent families. To hide my insecurity I became the class clown. At the same time I affected a feigned bravado with the other guys. The girls in my class at Friends had little or nothing to do with me. I imagined they considered me a bit of a ruffian. When I met Barbara she reminded me of the type of girl who would attend a private school, and that was part of why I was attracted to her.

Coincidentally, the day after the stockholder's meeting was the day before Barbara's birthday. My wife and I had been married for three years, but during the last year or so we had drifted apart. We still shared in the excitement of looking for antiques for our home, but Barbara's activities revolved mainly around her horses and the dog show world, which I detested. My wife felt fulfilled through her hobbies and her children. I, on the other hand, felt frustrated. Secretly, I had hoped my marriage would open a door into some sort of business deal—perhaps an association with the husband of one of Barbara's socially prominent friends—but after three years that had not materialized either.

It was impossible for me to express these feelings to anyone and, most unhappily, I saw no alternative to the life I was living. Married to a beautiful woman, I lived in a gracious country home, and, to top it all off, I was secure financially. After realizing what I imagined to be "The American Dream," I still felt inadequate, without real substance to my life.

During the month that elapsed between my purchase of the earthenware vessel and my Foote Mineral speech, I did not sit down with the whistle to pursue the intimation that had compelled me to buy the artifact. I treasured the little figurine, though, and tucked it away safely behind some books, high on a shelf in my study. Now and then I took the vessel down from its hiding place. I held it in my hands. I even blew into it a few times. I had not been mistaken that night at the auction; the whistle infused itself around my head. The sound was unlike anything I had ever heard before. What I felt was mysterious and compelling. Where would it lead me?

Let it be like wildflowers,
suddenly, an imperative
of the field.

— Yehuda Amechai

ALONE IN THE LIVING ROOM OF MY STATELY HOME, safely surrounded by my possessions, I took a deep breath and blew into the ancient vessel. For nearly a minute, the sustained, piercing note of the whistle enveloped my head. Again and again I repeated the process, immersing myself in the all-pervasive sound. I felt as if I were trying to drown out the thoughts of my failure ... as if somehow the sound would relieve me of having to face the emptiness of my life, with its trappings of a success that wasn't my own.

By the seventh or eighth breath, something happened. Suddenly, in the middle of an exhalation, my mind let go with a snap, and I perceived myself as a light. I had become a moving luminescence separate from what had been my physical body. As I traveled through a blue-black darkness, illuminating with my diffuse glow the path through which I moved, I sensed the space around me to be the universe.

I knew I was moving very fast—perhaps at the speed of light—

yet my sense of motion was not much different from my memory of driving down a country lane in a friend's Model-T Ford. Surprisingly, I was not afraid. This was a pleasant experience, exhilarating. Secure in my new form, I felt supported by the pulse of energy that had initiated my journey. Every now and then I passed other bodies of light; some were brighter than others. I thought of them either as planets or more distant stars. This new dimension seemed almost familiar. It did not occur to me to question whether or not I could return to my physical body.

I don't know in what direction or for how long I traveled in this manner, but suddenly I perceived an inky black cloud looming ahead. I sensed no way to avoid it, and although this apparition was no more strange than the rest of my experience, I was terror stricken. In what seemed an instant, my light body reached the edge of the odious form. I knew in my deepest core that unless I escaped at once I would be absorbed into the horrible blackness forever. As I touched the terrifying darkness, an explosive burst of energy reversed the direction of my travel. I crashed back into my body.

Back in my living room, I found myself sitting upright in a blue Martha Washington chair, still holding the ancient artifact in my hands. My heart was throbbing, and perspiration had soaked through my shirt. In a single moment I saw the enormity of my hypocrisy and the shallowness of my life. I saw the empty gesture and self-serving intent of returning the chromium mines to the black Africans, and my lowness in seeking to capitalize on the misfortunes of an oppressed people. I saw the futility in having married for money and social prestige, and the hurt I would inflict on Barbara and her children by breaking up their family once again. A sick feeling of guilt came over me; nothing I could do would relieve the pain I was about to cause. I also perceived—and this seemed the most terrible thing of all—that the horrible black cloud from which I had just narrowly escaped was the mirrored reflection, in my own soul, of the mean character of the people at the mining company whom I had accused of exploiting the black Africans. I was no different.

How could I ever change such a deeply rooted flaw in my character? What should I do (or could I do) about Barbara and the children now that I realized our life as a family was destined to end? When my heart stopped pounding, I walked out of my house and stood in the middle of the lawn that stretched from the front of the house to the river. The little estate was not mine at all; even though I legally owned the property, it never really had belonged to me. I was not the country squire I had pretended to be, but a short-term tenant. My pride had deluded me into thinking that, because I owned colonial objects and was married to a woman from the upper class, I too was cut from the same cloth ... or at least worthy of it. This was not the case, and no one besides me had believed it anyway. I had succeeded only in deluding myself. Vishnu could not have shattered his material world with the sound of his conch any more completely than the sound of that old whistle had shattered mine. My life as I had known it was over.

From a practical point of view, more time would be needed to accomplish what I had recognized in an instant. My first thought was that I should remain in the marriage for the sake of the children. Chip and Devon were only ten and eleven years old. Within a few years they would be teenagers, better able to withstand the shock of another family breakup. Besides, I was in no rush to go anywhere.

As best I could, I told my wife what had happened. She was incredulous and suggested we see a marriage counselor. Surely I had suffered some sort of mental hallucination. I had no *real* reason to go off aimlessly into the world when we *had* everything that any sane person would be grateful for: each other, the children, our beautiful home, and a comfortable life. Why would I want to give all that up?

I agreed to see the counselor, hoping she would be able to clarify the situation in a way that Barbara could better understand. Besides, I didn't have a good reason to go off aimlessly into the world when, by temporarily staying, I might ease the transition for everyone else.

Walking alone in nearby woods and fields, I began to see in a whole new way the natural world in which I lived. Gone were my schemes and the little typewritten cards that had obscured my view. I enjoyed the flowers as I never had before, breathing their colors into my body, as if they were some rare form of nourishment. I tasted the air. A steamy flavor arose in a boggy part of the meadow where a neighbor's cow had trampled the grass, and the woods behind the sawmill smelled nutty from moldering leaves mixed with sawdust. Textures and shades drew my attention: the jigsaw puzzle pattern in the bark of a Sycamore oak and the crinkle of a leaf afloat on a pond. All my senses were enhanced.

One afternoon I surprised a pheasant, which startled me with a whirr of wings as it flew from between my feet. Watching it fly across the field, I remembered a time when, as a young boy, I had found a pheasant killed by a hunter in Wilmington's Bringhurst Woods. The bird was unblemished except for a small smear of dried blood on its still-glistening feathers; I carried the pheasant home and carted it around the neighborhood in a metal washtub, half-expecting it would revive and fly away.

Now, twenty years later, I wondered why I had strayed from those simple pleasures. I had started with the usual teenage interests: cars, girls, and getting good enough grades to get into college. I had even enjoyed scouting. But along the way something had happened. Maybe the car accident that had kept me out of school for a year and prevented me from participating in sports had also pushed me out of the mainstream. In the tenth grade I bought a motorcycle and began to hang out with the older guys at the pool hall downtown. In my senior year I got a Mohawk haircut and graduated high school with a chip on my shoulder. After graduation I entered the University of Delaware, but dropped out after only a few weeks, joining the Merchant Marines and going to sea on an oil tanker. Within a month I was fired for being rebellious.

I tried a succession of jobs for the next couple of years, before my grandfather finally convinced me I wouldn't get anywhere in life without a college education. I completed college in three and a half years, and then joined my grandfather in the machine shop. My goal was to make enough money to get into politics and to find a wife who would further my prospects.

My experience with the whistle changed everything. Although no one suspected it, the person I had been until then ceased to exist. On April 27, 1972, I awoke anew.

Occasionally I would play the ancient instrument, hoping to initiate another vision. Nothing happened. It was impossible for me to leave my body again or to conjure up another insight. Although attempts to repeat my etheric journey were not successful, the sound still affected me. I would sit by the river and play the old vessel, concentrating on its piercing tone. Several breaths would immerse me in an ocean of sound, leaving me feeling refreshed and uplifted. My uncertainty would dissolve, carried away by the penetrating sound.

Discovering the culture that had produced my whistling bottle absorbed me. I enrolled in a night school class in anthropology and skimmed a shelf full of books on ethnographic art. I was able to identify my artifact as having been made by a pre-Inca Peruvian civilization. The seemingly dozens of cultures from different epochs, most of them with names I couldn't even pronounce, clouded my understanding.

I also initiated a formal study of the whistle's sound. The Franklin Institute in Philadelphia reported back to me that there wasn't anything particularly noteworthy about it. Their instruments determined it was just a loud whistle. In addition to the acoustical study, the people at the institute arranged with Hahnemann Hospital to conduct some biomedical tests. I was connected to an EKG machine, and my heart rate and blood pressure were measured while I blew into the artifact. I felt a little strange in the hospital, surrounded by lab technicians and one doctor, all wearing white hospital garb, watching me blow into an old black whistle. The technicians didn't find anything out of the ordinary in the physiological responses that they measured.

I was beginning to feel foolish.

It seemed as if I were running around on some kind of pseudo-scientific search, trying to find a rationale for what had happened, my actions only confirming Barbara's conclusion that I had suffered some sort of nervous breakdown. I was looking for a rational framework in which to place my experience, to explain the change in my perspective. I needed to define and validate it for myself and in terms that others could understand as well. Thinking that perhaps I could learn something from correspondences in other cultures, I began to read books and articles about meditation and spiritual practices.

I discovered that most cultures employ sound in their rituals to spark an impulse toward the Divine. The variety of sounds they use for this purpose, however, is bewildering. I read about Australian Aborigines who twirl a piece of carved bone or wood on the end of a string in order to make a humming sound that enables them to enter a trance. I learned about the Chistis, a school of Sufis who conduct meditative musical assemblies, increasing the fire of their devotion through specially evolved musical forms.

On the other side of the world, eleven Japanese priests circle an altar wearing heavy wood clogs on a wooden floor. One at a time they begin to run, very slowly at first, then faster and faster, until their running produces a thunder-like sound—twenty-two heavy percussion instruments, wood against wood. When the priests reach their highest speed, the first one throws one of his shoes against one of the wooden walls that surround the altar. The second priest throws his at a different point on the wall, and then the others follow, creating what sounds like twenty-two pistol shots, one after another. How had a ritual like that evolved, I wondered?

I remembered my surprise upon hearing the Shofar or ram's horn blown in the Jewish synagogue. Like a discordant trumpet, the harsh screech came unexpectedly in the midst of the ceremony, jolting my awareness out of the half-slumber the litany always induced. Perhaps the surprise was the point, I conjectured.

I bought a Folkways recording of Tibetan Buddhist religious music and listened to a cacophony of instruments that accompanied a group of monks who chanted traditionally prescribed chords to *resonate* into relationship with one or another of their deities. Part of their chant was sung in a deep, haunting melody, and every so often a trumpet, drum, or cymbal rang forth with a clashing sound as a sort of daemonic punctuation mark. I don't know what effect this had in Tibet, but in Pennsylvania the amplified sounds succeeded in driving Barbara out of the house for the afternoon.

Most interesting to me was the discovery of an East Indian practice. Categorized as a special psychological science or art, Mantra Yoga utilized specific sounds to attune the sacred union between the outer life and the deeper life of the initiate. The notes were secret, discovered over centuries by masters in India and communicated only to their disciples. I found the clearest elucidation of the mantra tradition in the book *Sri Aurobindo or the Adventure of Consciousness* by Sat Prem.

There exists in India a secret knowledge based on the study of sounds and the differences of vibratory modality according to the planes of consciousness. As each of our centers of consciousness is in direct communication with a plane, one can thus, by the repetition of certain sounds, put oneself in communication with the corresponding plane of consciousness. The basic or essential sounds that have the power of establishing this communication are called "mantra."

The mantras, always secret and given to the disciple by the Guru, are of all kinds and may serve the most contradictory ends. By the combination of certain sounds, one can, at lower levels of consciousness, generally at the vital level, put oneself into a relationship with the corresponding forces and obtain many strange powers. There are mantras that kill, mantras which attack with precision a particular part or organ of the body, mantras which heal, mantras which kindle fire, mantras which protect, and mantras that spell-bind.

On higher planes of consciousness, this kind of magic becomes poetry and music. There are also the spiritual mantras of the sacred writings and the mantras which the Guru gives his disciple to help him enter consciously into direct communication with one or another plane of consciousness, a particular force, or a specific divine being. The sound carries in itself the power of experience and realization. *It is a sound that makes one see!* (Italics added)

... Mantras, or sacred vibrations, may then be considered a powerful means for the opening of consciousness ... even initiation....[1]

This definition, I thought, could also apply to the Peruvian whistling bottle. As far as I was concerned, it too produced "sacred vibrations," perhaps designed for some sort of initiation. The vessel had affected me so profoundly that I was convinced it must have been intended for that purpose.

I wrote letters to dozens of anthropologists, archaeologists, and others whose areas of expertise seemed to touch on my experience. I asked everyone the same question: Do you know anything about a possible spiritual or ritual use for the whistling pots? Alfred Kidder, an anthropologist at the University of Pennsylvania, advised me that, as far as he knew, the whistling bottles were particular to the northwest coast of South America and had been catalogued as merely amusing liquid containers. Arthur Koestler wrote to me from London that he knew nothing about a ritual usage for the artifacts, but what I was describing reminded him of the "tingle" he experienced when hearing a bagpipe. Joseph Campbell wrote that I would have a very difficult time convincing the "academy" to reconsider their interpretation that the jugs were amusing liquid containers. He cautioned me, however, that if they did become interested, I would receive no credit from them for my hypothesis. Lévi-Strauss wrote to me from France that he found the idea interesting, but he too was unaware of anything that might corroborate my theory.

Finally I made a breakthrough in my quest. Dr. Junius Bird, curator emeritus of South American archaeology at the American Museum of Natural History, replied to my inquiry with an invitation to visit him in New York. Receiving Dr. Bird's letter was exciting. I was thrilled; here was an expert in the field who was actually willing to sit down and talk with me about the subject. I counted the days as my appointment with Dr. Bird approached, and carefully packed my artifact for our journey to New York.

An elderly gentleman with a fringe of snow-white hair greeted

me in an office on the fifth floor of the great museum. After introducing ourselves, we took the elevator back to the basement of
the building where the cafeteria was located. During lunch I related
my experience of finding and playing the old whistle, and my compelling desire to find out everything I could about it. I did not tell
Dr. Bird anything about my horrifying encounter with the black
cloud, but explained that I had had an "out of body" experience
that I felt had been catalyzed by the whistle.

"I've never heard of anything like that happening with one of
those bottles," the archaeologist stated after I had completed my
story. "With San Pedro cactus or one of the other hallucinogen-
ics like Ayahuasca, yes, but not a whistling bottle. In fact, I don't
recall any mention of them ever being 'played.'"

"Are there many whistling pots known?" I asked.

"Yes, they're fairly common in museum collections," he answered.
"The Meso and South American people made an enormous variety of pottery, but the whistling bottles were made almost exclusively in the Andean area. A few have been found at archaeological
sites in Mexico, but those are constructed differently than the ones
from the Andean area ... from Colombia in the north to southern Peru is where they're mainly found."

"How long were they made?" I inquired.

"At least two thousand years," Dr. Bird answered, almost casu-
ally. "Perhaps as early as 1000 B.C. and then continuously until
shortly after the Spanish conquest in 1532. The very earliest examples appear in the north, in Colombia. By 500 B.C., whistle pots
turn up on the north coast of what is now Peru."

"Then they were made for twenty-five hundred years!" I exclaimed, surprised at what seemed to me a very long period of
time for the enigmatic vessels to have persisted.

"Yes," he answered, unperturbed by my surprise. "We know that
whistle pots were made after the conquest as well because we've

found a few examples that had been glazed. Pottery glazes were introduced by the Spanish," he explained.

"Is anything specifically known about these vessels?" I asked. "Anything that indicates a possible spiritual or ritual usage for them?"

"I can't recall any mention of it, but new discoveries are constantly being made, especially with so many ethnologists working with the Indians now. I don't remember reading anything about the whistle pots, though, in the accounts of the chroniclers. The chroniclers were mainly missionary priests." Dr. Bird thought about it for a moment longer. "No, I can't recall ever coming across any mention that suggests a ritual use for them."

"Dr. Kidder told me the whistle feature was constructed as an amusing air vent," I volunteered. "He said that unless there was an extra hole in the top—something like the little hole on the top of a gasoline can—the vessel would air-lock and be impossible to fill with liquid. The current interpretation of the whistle is that an ingenious potter discovered he could attach a whistle to the vent hole. It was such an amusing device that from then on other potters continued to perpetuate it."

"My old friend Adrian Digby wrote the article proposing that explanation," Dr. Bird laughed. "Here, I've dug the article out for you to look at." The archaeologist handed me a large hardbound book with the imposing title, *29th International Congress of Americanists: Selected Papers.* "I must say, though, that poor Digby was forced to write this sort of paper in those days."

"What do you mean by that?" I asked.

"You see," Dr. Bird explained, "Digby worked at the British Museum. The administrators there would never give the poor man any money to travel to our conferences. So Adrian would write about something every year or so, usually on some obscure topic that hadn't been covered in the literature, and submit his article to the Congress of Americanists. When he was invited to present his paper, the British Museum would pay for his trip. I remember Adrian giving his talk on that subject. It was here in New York, a few years after the war. 1949, I believe. In the old days it was much more difficult to get funding to travel to conventions, and God knows our salaries wouldn't have begun to cover it."

I told Dr. Bird I had commissioned the Franklin Institute to analyze the sound of my whistling pot. "So far they haven't found anything special about it. The engineer who's working on it says it's just a loud whistle."

"Perhaps if you measured a larger sample of vessels you would find something," he suggested. "Why don't you bring your engineer up here and test the whistles in our collection?"

"I could do that?" I asked, surprised at the archaeologist's invitation.

"Yes, of course," he replied. "Let's take a walk over to the storeroom where we keep our collection. Very little of what we have here in the museum is on display in the public galleries. Most of it is in storage."

Dr. Bird led me down the corridor to the storeroom and unlocked a nondescript wooden door with a key. Then the archaeologist flipped a wall switch to turn on the lights. I wasn't prepared for the sight before me. The room was small, perhaps twelve feet square and ten feet high, stacked from floor to ceiling with shelves that overflowed with ceramics from ancient Peru. Hundreds of globular vessels crowded the dusty shelves. The sculpted heads of warriors, priests, and chieftains, lifelike with their eyes painted open and softly modeled features, gazed down at me. Clay death masks, through hollow eye sockets and vacant stares, transported their message from centuries past. I saw faces ravaged by disease. I saw clay figurines of couples in erotic embrace. I saw the sellers of herbs in the market and the fishermen who had set sail on their last voyage. I saw disembodied hands, feet, and penises ... vegetables, monkeys, and birds, all modeled in clay in exquisite detail. The assembly of effigies was a portrait, captured in clay, of an entire civilization. I was dumbfounded by the enormity of it all.

Dr. Bird broke the silence. "This has been my life's work," he said, making a sweeping gesture with his arm to encompass the room. "Although I specialize in the textiles, I never tire of seeing the ceramics. After a while you begin to recognize the characters and personae that appear time and again in these people's art. Now some of these ghosts almost seem like old friends," he chuckled.

"How do you sort all of this—I mean, how do you organize it into something understandable?" I stammered, trying to comprehend the collection in front of me. I was more than curious. The room full of artifacts was overwhelming, and I felt touched in a way I didn't understand, as if I had once known the people represented by the clay figurines. Of course that was impossible, even with the wildest notions of genetic memory. My ancestry was Eastern European, not South American.

"Archaeologists identify the various Andean cultures through their pottery," Dr. Bird was already answering. "For instance, the flared lip on the spout of this blackware piece indicates it was made by the Incas. A Chimú potter on the north coast would have made the same artifact, but with a straight spout. This chalky-white pottery, usually decorated with a simple black or brown pigment, we call 'Chancay' for the area where it's found. This true-to-life painted portrait vase we identify as 'Mochica' or 'Moche,' once again, named for the principal river valley where it is found.

"Stylistic differences do not always indicate a difference in geography," he added. "For instance, the Mochica inhabited the same river valleys as the Chimú, but earlier. Later, when the Chimú were absorbed into the Inca Empire, their pottery changed to reflect design elements that were typically Inca. It takes a bit of study to see the picture, but once you're familiar with it you'll recognize similar themes portrayed in the art of every culture. *All* of these cultures made whistling bottles," Dr. Bird concluded.

As we walked back to the curator's office, I was quiet. I wondered how the little whistles attached to some of these ancient effigies could have been accidental, functioning only as amusing air vents. I had played one of these instruments, and it had transported me through a field of stars. I had experienced a horrific encounter while traveling through the universe, and I had seen a deep truth, however horrible, within myself. Perhaps Digby's explanation was too simple. Regardless of the academic interpretation, I would pursue my intimation further.

Chimú whistling vessel: circa 1000–1400 A.D.

Three Chimú whistling vessels: circa 1000–1500 A.D.

Two Huari/Chimú whistling vessels: circa 1000–1200 A.D.

Two Vicus whistling vessels: circa 300 B.C.–100 A.D.

Two Salinar whistling vessels: circa 500–300 B.C.

Moche/Chimú whistling vessel: circa 900–1100 A.D.

Two Inca whistling vessels: circa 1300–1400 A.D.

Chimú/Lambayequi whistling vessel: circa 1000–1300 A.D.

Three Chancay whistling vessels: circa 1200–1400 A.D.

Machu Picchu: view from the Inca Trail leading into the city.

Life is not a problem to be solved, it is a mystery
to be lived.

—*Søren Kierkegaard*

M Y ENCOUNTER WITH THE GALLERY OF FACES sculpted in clay added another dimension to my own artifact. Although the people portrayed on the ceramics were not recognizable to me as individuals, they were familiar in the same way as are the people pictured in an old box of photographs found in a grandparent's attic. My Chimú vessel was only a single portrait from an extensive cultural family. Why did I feel such a deep connection to a people so distant from my own ancestry?

Two weeks later I returned to New York with Bill Hargens, the engineer who was studying the acoustical properties of my whistle at the Franklin Institute. Upon arriving at the museum, we were led by one of Dr. Bird's assistants to the storeroom of ancient Peruvian ceramics.

Enough space had been left in the center of the crowded floor to maneuver a ladder, which I climbed to reach the upper shelves. Methodically, I collected the whistling bottles from each shelf. Working slowly, I enjoyed the sight and feel of each artifact. When I came across one I would blow into it to make sure that its whistle was intact before handing it down to Hargens, who had set up his equipment in a room across the hall.

The silver-and-black sound spectrum analyzer seemed alien in the midst of the ancient clay figurines. Could the whistles' elusive quality ever be captured by the instrument's wires and quantified by its dials? I blew into one of the whistles while Hargens took preliminary measurements to calibrate his equipment. The engineer found that the location in the room where the whistles were loudest was contiguous to my ear when I was blowing into the instrument. (Unlike typical musical instruments, whistling pots were constructed so that the sounds were directed back toward the person who was blowing into them.)

Hargens then proceeded to measure the frequency and loudness of each vessel I had selected. The pots came to life with a piercing tone, nearly equal in loudness to that of my original instrument. But there was nothing acoustically distinctive about any of them; they were just loud whistles ... except for one: a double-chambered, globular vessel made of gray-black earthenware. As with my first whistle, one chamber was modeled around a spout; the other was a large cylinder (like a drum) with a pair of owls perched on its rim. One owl was slightly larger than the other, giving the impression they were a male and female couple. Both birds appeared to be in a state of repose; I imagined them to be content. I blew into the vessel's spout, and the sound filled my head.

Hargens told me the whistle was very loud, over 100 decibels, and its tone was particularly rich in harmonic partials. The partials gave the whistle an extra dimension of fullness, of timbre. The sound engineer explained that harmonic partials are "overtones," a sequence of higher tones proportionally related to the fundamental or basic pitch. Partials are not nearly as loud as the fundamental frequency, but they can be heard. The owl whistle had at least five partials that Hargens could identify with his mobile equipment.

"There might even be more of them," he remarked. "But they would be in the ultrasonic range, inaudible to the human ear."

"Does the brain perceive ultrasonic sounds?" I asked him.

"A 'Frequency Following Response' occurs in the brain," he answered. "That's electrical activity in response to acoustical stimulation. But I don't know of any specific response to ultrasonic sounds. The interesting thing about this group of whistles is that their tones are clustered together in a narrow range of frequencies. They could easily have encompassed a much wider range than they do. It's puzzling."

"Does this prove that the vessels were made intentionally? Does this prove that they were pitched to make these exact sounds?" I asked him.

"No," he answered. "You can't prove that these whistles were intentionally pitched by measuring less than a dozen of them made by two or three cultures. You'd need a sample much more controlled than that."

"This was made by the Chimú," Dr. Bird pronounced, when I was once again seated in his office. The Andean scholar carefully placed my treasure in a small clearing amidst the piles of books and papers on his desk, and leaned back in his well-worn swivel chair.

"They're long gone," he mused, almost to himself. "The Chimú civilization that is," he added. Removing his wire-rimmed spectacles, the archaeologist began to clean them with a white cloth handkerchief.

"Who were they?" I asked, curious to know how the old whistle had found its way to me in Pennsylvania.

"The Chimú were the rulers of a vast kingdom," he answered. "Now we identify their particular cultural horizon by that name.

The Chimú kingdom stretched for more than six hundred miles along the northwest coast of what is now Peru. To give you an idea, it encompassed a territory that was equivalent in size to the populated area of California from San Diego to San Francisco. Millions of people created an extensive civilization with a highly developed agricultural and political state. They were great builders and engineers, metalworkers and weavers. People from that area were weaving intricate designs into their textiles five hundred years before the Egyptians even domesticated cotton."

Dr. Bird carefully removed a little black case from his desk drawer. Nestled in cotton batting, behind a piece of glass that served as the case's cover, was an exquisite llama, the Peruvian camel, cast in gold. Next to the llama was the tiny figurine of a woman, also made of gold. Even without experience in such matters, I clearly could see the quality in the finely wrought precious objects.

"These were cast by the 'lost wax' method," the curator told me. "Lost wax is a metallurgical process that was discovered and perfected by an Andean craftsman. It's an outstanding achievement in metalworking. The artisan began by making an exact wax model of this llama, much as a sculptor works in clay," he explained. "The wax came from the stingless bees of the rain forest; it was mixed with tree sap such as copal gum to make it workable. The artisan then attached a cone of wax to his little sculpture; the wax cone later served as a funnel in which to pour the molten metal. When the wax model was complete the artist painted it with powdered charcoal mixed with water. That's what gives the cast figurines such a smooth surface," he added.

"The next step in the process was to cover the model with an outer shell made from a mixture of moist clay and crushed charcoal. This had to be done without covering the pouring funnel or disturbing the little wax rods that were attached to the model to serve as air vents. After the outer shell dried the entire assembly was fired. This strengthened the mold, burning out the wax and leaving a cavity of the same shape and volume as the now-lost wax model. The mold was then brought to a red heat to facilitate the flow of molten metal, and was placed with the pouring channel uppermost. Then the molten gold was poured in. When the gold solidified, the mold was broken away to reveal a metal figure of the wax original. The excess metal in the pouring channel and the rods that had formed in the air vents were cut off and the cuts were smoothed over. The finished object was then polished; that was the final step in the process."

"Was the artisan able to reuse the mold to make more figurines?" I asked.

"No, only one," he answered.

"What you've described sounds like a lot of work to produce a single statue," I said. "If anything went wrong the artist would have to start all over again, carve a new model out of wax. Every sculpture was unique." The gold figurine of the llama and the little gold stature of the woman somehow seemed more important to me now that I knew they were the only ones exactly like them in the world.

"Andean craftsmen made bimetallic objects as well, casting metals with a lower melting point such as silver around a metal with a higher melting point such as gold," he added. "The ancient technique was the forerunner of modern metal 'cladding.'"

"Where did these people learn these metallurgical processes?" I asked.

"No one knows," Dr. Bird replied, "but specialists have advanced two views. The first view is that the Andean people were capable of independently discovering these techniques for themselves. The second position purports that the processes are so complex, they must have been imported from across the Pacific. No concrete evidence supports either contention.

"Pre-Columbian textiles were equally wonderful, equal to the best European tapestries. Look at this fragment," he added, showing me a small piece of cloth about eight inches square that was also mounted in a glass frame. On a brilliant gold background, a ruby-red cat with a long stylized tail stared out at me. Within the cat's belly another, smaller cat reclined, and within that cat still another tinier cat was embroidered. Disconcertingly, all three pairs of cats' eyes were human in appearance.

"How did you re-dye the fabric?" I asked, impressed with the brightness of the brilliant hues in the cloth.

"This hasn't been re-dyed," Dr. Bird answered. "In fact, it hasn't even been cleaned. This cloth was woven before the birth of Christ, perhaps as early as 500 B.C."

"But how could that be?" I asked. "Everything deteriorates, especially fabric." The Andean scholar was telling me that two thousand, five hundred years after being woven, the cloth square in front of me was not only perfectly preserved, but was also as brightly colored as anything I had ever seen. I was incredulous.

"This fragment is from a large cache of fabrics that were found in a cave on the Paracas Peninsula," the archaeologist continued. "The region is extremely dry, and this cloth was woven to be interred with a burial—a burial not in the earth, but above ground, in a cave. Without exposure to sunlight or moisture, the fibers haven't deteriorated. Paracas Necropolis textiles are probably the finest weavings in the world."

"You'd think that something crafted this early would be much less advanced," I said. "The mastery of any craft usually evolves over time."

"That's not the case with the Peruvian material," Dr. Bird answered. "The earliest pottery is often of the highest quality, and although the later textiles are quite wonderful in their own right, the original Paracas is undoubtedly the finest expression of the weavers' art.

"What this implies is that an even earlier progression or development in the arts exists of which we're not yet aware. Because of the fragility of the materials and the great length of time, very little has survived from that earliest period when weaving and pottery first evolved. As far as the cultures that we have identified, from about 500 B.C. through 1500 A.D., we see real degeneration. Your Chimú pot here, which was probably made sometime between 1200 A.D. and 1500 A.D., is very clumsy compared to Mochica pottery, which was made in the same river valleys but a couple of hundred years earlier. Anthropologists believe these various cultures were distinct from one another, but the design elements and themes were universal to the region. This indicates a common heritage or linkage of the various Andean cultures."

"What became of the Chimú?" I asked. "I never heard of them before I bought this whistle pot."

"They were absorbed into the Inca Empire less than a hundred years before the Spanish arrival—1471, I believe. The Chimú weren't a distinct race any more than were the Incas," Dr. Bird explained. "In fact, the word *Chimú,* like the word *Inca,* originally referred to the imperial rulers of their respective territories. The two regions were different in other ways—language, for instance. The Incas spoke 'Quechua' while the Chimú spoke 'Mochica.' When the Chimú were absorbed into the Inca Empire they became Quechua speakers. Mochica is now an extinct language. No one has spoken it for centuries."

In the midst of the scholar's explanation, the idea occurred to me that the sound of my Chimú whistle had survived long after the last words of an entire people had faded into the silence of eternity. Perhaps the enigmatic artifacts were a transmission across the centuries, I mused, a legacy that transcended language. My artifact had survived the dispersion of genes and syllables, and the erosion of time, for nearly a thousand years.

"What we know of the Chimú comes from oral tradition, transcribed by a Spanish priest." Dr. Bird continued. "After a long succession of rulers their kingdom was finally conquered by the Incas."

"How did that happen?" I asked. "Weren't they a powerful nation as well?"

"Actually, *persuaded* would be a better word to use than *conquered*," he replied. "The Inca army did not attack the Chimú militarily. Instead, the army marched into the mountains above the Chimú capital city of Chan-Chan and diverted the primary river that supplied water to the capital. As he watched his people's lifeline rushing uselessly into the desert, the last Chimú King, a man named Minchanzaman, surrendered his realm to the Incas."

"He surrendered just for the water?" I asked.

"It's not *just* water there," Dr. Bird replied. "The north coast of Peru is very, very dry—arid. It rains there perhaps twice in a century. Imagine: Only a single rainfall in a man's lifetime. Without the river, no human habitation could exist. Chan-Chan may even have had a water-based economy," he added. "A man's wealth would have depended on the amount of water he was allotted."

"That sounds like a science fiction story I once read," I interjected.

"It's not science fiction," Dr. Bird replied with a smile. "Minchanzaman was the ultimate authority, presiding over the allocation of water as well as disputes. Remember, water was his country's primary resource. Stealing even a small amount of it would have been a serious offense. The sovereign may have had to punish men who broke the law. In pre-Columbian times, punishment included stoning to death, hanging, and banishment. These punishments were meted out for what we might consider minor offenses. Imagine, then, the enormity of seeing the entire river diverted into the desert."

The archaeologist paused in his discourse, and I tried to imagine what he had just described. It was hard for me to picture the Chimú king surrendering to the Incas for the return of their river, but if the monarch had sentenced men to death for taking more than their share.... Dr. Bird answered the telephone on his desk, had a brief conversation, then returned his attention to me.

"Two other imposing ruins dominate the Moche River Valley, the *Huaca del Sol,* and the *Huaca de la Luna,* or Pyramids of the Sun and the Moon. Both are colossal structures, constructed from millions of adobe bricks. Words can barely convey their size. Before the Spanish diverted the Moche River against the edifice in search of gold, the *Huaca del Sol* was believed to be the largest adobe structure in the world."[1]

"It's interesting that first the Incas diverted the river to capture the Chimú kingdom. Then the Spanish diverted the river to search for treasure," I reflected. "The real treasure was the river itself. What does the word *huaca* mean?" I asked.

"It's more than a word," Dr. Bird answered. "Actually, it's a generic term that means a holy or sacred thing. A *huaca* was anything in which the Indians discerned something of the supernatural. They applied the word to special rocks, springs, mountains, and caves—in fact, to anything in which they intuited an aura of sanctity. Ancient ruins, especially burial places and pre-Columbian artifacts such as your whistle here—even certain constellations associated with mythological happenings—were considered 'charged' with a transcendent memory. A *huaca* was empowered with a spirit because of its earlier association.

"An Inca descendent, Garcilaso de la Vega, wrote that the original sense of the word *huaca* was 'to weep,'" the archaeologist continued. "Viracocha, the Andean creator-hero, by far the most celebrated mythical being in the chronicles of ancient Peru, is also known as 'the weeping god.'"

"How does that tie in with the *huacas?*" I asked.

"I don't know whether it ties in or not," Dr. Bird answered. "The legend surrounding Viracocha is that first he created heaven and earth and then caused the sun and moon to rise out of Lake Titicaca. The story continues that Viracocha then fashioned normal-sized men out of clay, breathed life into them, and then...."

"Excuse me," I interrupted. "The Peruvian legend of Creation holds that the first men were made out of clay and their Creator 'breathed' life into them. Why that's exactly what the potter did when he made this whistling pot," I said enthusiastically. "Surely the making of this pottery was a re-enactment or some sort of metaphor for the potter's own creation by Viracocha. It's a direct correlation with the root belief of the Andean people."

"Not so fast, young man," Dr. Bird admonished. "We haven't gotten that far yet. Until we know for certain, we cannot say in what context this vessel was regarded by the people who made it."

"I can see why 'weeping' may have been considered a primary attribute of the god," I declared, my mind skipping ahead. "Weeping is the expressed idealization of the free flow of emotions—both joy as well as sorrow—that could have served as an example of integrity and wholeness. A weeping god might represent an ideogram for absolute honesty of feeling and expression."

"That would make an interesting article," the museum curator commented, "although highly speculative. Even if you could get it published, I doubt whether anyone in the field would take you seriously." Dr. Bird resumed his explanation.

"My sense of the word huaca is that the term is not limited to religion as we define it, but rather reflects a concept indicative of a spiritual worldview. Remember, the conquest took place in the sixteenth century. Spanish clerics came to the New World with a hierarchical view that separated what was material from what was considered spiritual. On the other hand, the Indians saw no such separation. Everything was connected back and forth through the heavens and the earth with a spirit inextricably woven throughout the whole of Creation," Dr. Bird concluded.

"So the descendants of the people who actually made this vessel consider it to be a sacred object," I reiterated. "Yet anthropologists catalogue its whistle as merely an amusing air vent. Why, this pot is a *huaca!*"

As I drove home to Pennsylvania, my mind raced with excitement from the conversation I'd had with Dr. Bird. Despite the museum curator's admonition regarding my speculations, I decided to write an article. For months I wrote diligently and continuously, correlating and synthesizing varied and diverse information about meditation, pre-Columbian history and the effects of sound on consciousness. With single-minded determination, I organized my findings into a semblance of coherence. The resultant article was my attempt to construct a framework in which to place my experience with the old clay whistle, to articulate a rationale for what had occurred in my life, and to explain my change in perception and direction.

At the same time I was writing this exposition, my personal life was in upheaval. Months of counseling had guided Barbara and me to the obvious but painful conclusion that we needed to go in different directions. I saw the dissolution of our marriage as an attempt to heal an aspect of the black reflection I had encountered during my journey of light. The terrifying object I had so despairingly touched was linked directly to my selfish, materialistic desires. Finally I was able to admit to myself and to Barbara that, for me, our marriage was based mainly on social and material concerns. Disentanglement from my business schemes paralleled the dissolution of my marriage. Both were facets of the same disease, and, as I struggled to break free from the materialism represented by each, I felt as if I were shedding a cumbersome weight with which I alone had burdened myself.

Ostensibly, I wrote a thesis based on my experience with the pottery whistle. My "journey of light" had brought about a vision of universal harmony. This is what had catalyzed my persevering research into the archaic Chimú vessel, I wrote in my article. The truth was another matter altogether. Ashamed of what I had seen within myself, I was unable to tell anyone what had really occurred, let alone write about it. The final version of my article glossed over the actual event that had initiated my passionate quest. In a few short sentences, I reduced the most profoundly important experience of my adult life to a falsified story of harmony and well-being.

In 1974 I learned of a journal that published articles about mystical and altered states of consciousness. I sent them my story and they accepted it for publication. The *Journal of Transpersonal Psychology* is a publication serving a readership of psychologists and educators who support the idea that many of the so-called psychopathologies are, in fact, transpersonal experiences. The "transpersonal" is defined as a state of consciousness characterized by transcendence of the individual ego boundary. People who experience a transpersonal state no longer regard themselves as separate and isolated from their surroundings; rather, they see themselves as intimately woven into the fabric of a greater reality.

The hypothesis advanced by the Transpersonal Association is that the basis for many of the unusual perceptions reported by people is actually a deep evolutionary impulse toward transformation. From this perspective, transpersonal experiences are not indicative of mental disorder, but may be viewed as a legitimate opportunity for growth. In most Western cultures, however, people who have such experiences are misunderstood because of the absence of an acceptable cultural framework in which to place their experience. As a result of the alarm they occasion, many of these people end up in mental hospitals or under the care of a psychiatrist.

One of them was loose in Pennsylvania, running around the woods with an ancient whistle.

In the final days before publication of the issue that contained my article, I clearly saw the dishonesty with which I had characterized my experience. Conscious-stricken, I telephoned the publisher, Anthony Sutich, in California to confess my pretense. I had never spoken to Mr. Sutich prior to this call. I felt an imperative to tell him the truth, however, before my words were indelibly etched in printer's ink.

"Mr. Sutich, this is Daniel Stat,"[2] I said, introducing myself. "I'm the person who wrote the article about my experience with the ancient Peruvian whistle."

"I enjoyed your article, Daniel," Mr. Sutich replied. "What can I do for you?"

I stammered for a moment, unable to find the words I needed. Having labored so carefully to articulate my story, it was ironic that now, in speaking to the publisher, I just needed to speak the plain truth. I've forgotten exactly what I said, but I was able to confess to Mr. Sutich that the feeling of unity and harmony I had described in my article was actually a deep encounter with the darkest and most horrible aspect of myself. I also told the publisher that writing the story was not much more than the expression of my need to rationalize and justify my experience.

Finally I had told someone the truth, even though it was over the phone and to a man I didn't know. I let out a deep breath, probably more of a sigh, and listened to the silence from three thousand miles away.

At last Mr. Sutich broke the silence. "Daniel," he began, "I'm going to publish the article the way it is. Your personal insight is only a part of the story. As far as what you've just told me, we can keep that between the two of us."

The publisher's words pierced my disquiet. On some essential level Mr. Sutich had forgiven me for what I had done or seen within myself. I didn't know which. His decision to publish my article was the deep acceptance that I had unknowingly been in search of. I felt as if an enormous load had been lifted from my shoulders, and words were inadequate to express my gratitude. I know that somehow I stammered, "Thank you, sir. Thank you very much."

Earth's million roads struggled towards Deity.

—*Sri Aurobindo*

THE FIRST NIGHT ON THE ROAD I slept in Columbus, right in front of the big statue of Christopher. I had driven all day. It was nearly midnight before I pulled off the highway and parked on a downtown street. Turning off the ignition, I listened to the motor fade into silence. Then I climbed into the camper on the back of the truck. Before I fell asleep, I thought about the events that had precipitated the remarkable change in my life. Only a moment ago I had been a country squire. Now, in the fall of 1975, I had just crawled into bed in a camper on the back of an old Chevy pickup truck, parked on an unfamiliar street in Columbus, Ohio.

It had taken three years since my encounter with the black cloud to disentangle the web of artifice that I had made of my life. But I had finally gathered enough courage to leave the security of my marriage and the community that had been my home for my entire adult life.

Now I was headed for California. I had no job, no profession, only an unshakable conviction that I had been chosen to decipher and make known the meaning of the old whistle that had summoned my insight. I had been given a second chance in life by a Chimú vessel, or by a priest or wizard who centuries before had empowered it. My reading had confirmed Junius Bird's assertion regarding the Indian belief in a spiritual reality that pervaded the whole of existence. Historians' accounts, without exception, agreed, "In Peru everything was alive. The smallest object had a soul: the llama and the potato, the rock and the individual."[1] Father Cobo's extensive list of *huacas* included rivers, springs, and lakes, each with its own spirit requiring acknowledgment and reaffirmation throughout the year.[2]

But it was the story of the Andean Creation legend that I had learned from Dr. Bird that tied it all together for me. Clay and breath were the primordial elements in man's creation. According to the people who had inhabited Peru, human beings were comprised of earth that had been animated by the breath of the Creator. *Alpacamasca,* the Inca word for a person's body, means "animated earth."

The images washed over me: animated earth ... a spirit in the water ... the first men formed from clay ... rekindling the sacred fire.... All, elements combined by the potter and modeled into a vessel that would become "animated" itself when its creator blew into it. Could the making and the playing of the earthenware pots have been anything other than a metaphor—perhaps some sort of re-enactment—of the Peruvian Indian's own Creation? How could it have been otherwise?

I had bought a second Chimú whistle pot from the widow of a collector in Greenwich Village. I bought a third at an auction of pre-Columbian art in Manhattan, after my visit to Dr. Bird. The widow's whistle pot was double-chambered, its form much like my original except that the figure was clownish in appearance, with a round little body and smallish head topped with a tall conical hat. The other vessel portrayed a tiny man riding upon a raft made of gourds. Both artifacts were made of the same black clay as my first one. They smelled as if they had been buried in the earth for centuries.

The day that I bought them, I tried to play the whistles simultaneously in my hotel room across the street from the auction gallery in New York. I couldn't manage to blow into both vessels at the same time, so I asked Barbara, who had accompanied me to New York for the weekend, to play one of the old whistles along with me. She viewed my request with mild dismay, but agreed to humor me after I had thoroughly washed the spout of the whistle I had asked her to play. It took a little practice, but finally we were playing the two whistles together at full blast. The effect was astonishing. An otherworldly sound engulfed the room, as if a cyclone or whirlwind had arrived in the middle of Manhattan. Beginning as a low rumble, the sound rose rapidly in pitch to become a full-blown maelstrom that sounded like a swarm of bees. But it was a swarm of bees buzzing around the *inside* of my head.

We played several breaths together in this fashion, and with each breath the strange sound reappeared, flooding my brain with its distinct sensation. I actually could *feel* the sound traveling from one side of my head to the other, like a gentle massage of my brain. I felt as if waves of energy were washing my mind, sweeping away my thoughts. I had never experienced anything like it. Barbara, too, heard strange sounds, but the sensation did not astonish her as it did me. In those moments in our hotel room on Madison Avenue, I knew that the vessels had been made as instruments of mysterious purpose, and that somehow I was being led to rediscover their purpose.

It wasn't just the strange sounds that caused me to believe I had made a discovery. I had been touched in a way that transcended my rational mind. The depths that had opened to me through the sound of the old whistles was immeasurably valuable, a value that far exceeded the riches I'd hoped to gain through my business schemes.

I began to share the whistles with friends from Wilmington and learned that everyone could at least hear the strange sounds. Most said the phenomenon had a centering or calming effect, clearing their mind of thoughts and leaving them with a spacious feeling in which new ideas could emerge. This strengthened my conviction that originally the vessels had been intended for some psycho-logical or psycho-spiritual technology that had been lost or hidden in the dark ages of the Spanish conquest.

As I drifted off to sleep in my pickup truck in Columbus, I thought briefly of the man for whom the city was named. He, too, had journeyed west, following the sun in pursuit of his dream. The next morning I drove to St. Louis. The great arch, shimmering in the late afternoon sun, seemed indeed the "gateway to the West."

Driving across the Kansas plains and into Colorado, I remembered making the same drive with my parents when I was ten years old. It had been our first extended family vacation. Dad drove the big four-door sedan while Mom tended to my younger sister and brother who were then seven and four years old. I could recall walking along the top rail of a wooden fence next to a motel. I could also remember seeing my first drive-in movie, *Giant,* somewhere in Iowa. Colorado provided the most vivid memory of the trip. We rented a "real" cabin in the Rockies outside of Denver, and my dad lit the wood stove by flicking a blue-tip match with his thumbnail to ignite the flame. It was the first time I'd seen him do something like that, and I was impressed. In Denver, we ate the best fried chicken in the world. At least that's what the restaurant's sign proclaimed. The waitress told Mom that the secret ingredient in the batter was corn flakes. When we reached California we stayed with relatives in Long Beach. I remember going to the Pike amusement park, and panning for gold at Knott's Berry Farm. Hastily, we returned to the east coast, when some business crisis needed Dad's attention.

Now, at age thirty-two, I sensed California would be a place where I could let go of my past and begin a new life. It was also a place where I could fully explore the ramifications of my discovery. From reports I'd read, California was the American proving ground for new ideas. The Peruvian whistles would find a niche there, and so would I.

A week or so after my arrival in Los Angeles, I drove to UCLA to introduce myself to an assistant professor of Andean studies with whom I had developed a correspondence. Dr. Christopher Donnan had graciously responded to my initial letter about the whistles. He was intrigued by my theory that the sounds had been specifically pitched and that the vessels may have been intended as instruments. I found Dr. Donnan's office on the third floor of Haines Hall. A small card on the door informed me that the professor's office hours would begin later that morning.

"Good morning, Dr. Donnan," I said extending my hand toward the light-haired assistant professor who beckoned me into his office. "I'm Daniel Stat," I said, introducing myself. "I wrote to you some time ago about my discovery of a Chimú whistle at an auction in Pennsylvania."

"Yes, I remember your letter," Dr. Donnan replied with a friendly smile. "For some reason, though, I had the impression that you were a farmer and a much older man. Please sit down," he said, pointing to a chair next to his desk.

"I've just moved to Los Angeles and I wanted to meet you," I said, somewhat at a loss for how to proceed. "My sister lives here and I've moved in with her. I'm still very interested in whistling vessels," I continued. "Since writing the article I sent you, I've discovered a unique acoustical effect that occurs when several of the instruments are played together. In fact, I've been invited to demonstrate the effect at a seminar for graduate students at Columbia University."

"What sort of effect is it?" Dr. Donnan asked.

"It's hard for me to put into words," I answered. "The sounds somehow combine in a unique way. You can actually 'feel' them, almost in the same way that you feel someone's touch on your skin. I've left my whistles on the east coast in anticipation of my presentation there," I explained, "or I'd demonstrate the effect for you."

"Why don't we continue this conversation downstairs, in my museum office?" Dr. Donnan suggested. "Since our correspondence, I've been appointed Director of UCLA's Museum of Cultural History."

"What sort of museum is it, Dr. Donnan?" I asked.

"Why don't you call me Chris?" the young professor asked graciously. "To answer your question, the Museum of Cultural History is an extensive collection of ethnographic and archaeological materials. Every day the university receives donations of artifacts that alumni or people in the community have collected and no longer want. Most of it ends up here at Haines Hall."

"Is it on exhibit?" I asked.

"No," Chris answered. "Our museum is primarily a study museum utilized by scholars. Individual rooms house artifacts from various cultures. Sometimes a room encompasses a geographic area with various cultures. For example, Mexico and South America are combined in one room. I'm certain, though, that we have examples of the whistling bottles here," Chris remarked as he unlocked a wooden door that led into one of the storerooms in the basement of the building.

Once again I was in immediate contact with a room full of artifacts made by the people who had devised my whistle. As Dr. Donnan had surmised, a number of whistles from the Chimú and Inca cultures were included in the collection.

"Let's take a few of them back to my office," Chris suggested, handing me a brown cardboard box. Selecting five or six of the black earthenware vessels, we carried them back to Dr. Donnan's museum office, where he called together several members of his staff.

"This is Daniel Stat," Chris said, introducing me to the museum's registrar, photographer, and several secretaries whom he had invited into his spacious office.

"Daniel has a theory that whistling bottles were originally intended to be played as instruments. I've asked him to demonstrate their effect," Dr. Donnan explained, indicating that I should begin.

"I believe these vessels were employed as mind-altering tools by the people who devised them," I began. Blowing into one of the vessels, I demonstrated the amount of breath required to produce a loud, clear tone. "Too much pressure," I cautioned, "makes the whistle inoperable. If you don't blow hard enough, the tone won't reach its optimal pitch."

Everyone tentatively blew an experimental breath or two into his or her vessel to get the feel of it. Then we began to play together. We may as well have been playing the whistles that I had left on the east coast. This random selection of instruments from the UCLA museum created exactly the same effect. Once again, it seemed as if a powerful wind had entered the room with the combined sounds of the old instruments. The effect was immediate and dramatic. Even though I had experienced it a number of times, I was still affected by the unique phenomenon. I sensed that the people in the room were inwardly moved, as well. They appeared reserved, however, and somewhat reluctant to express their feelings.

Finally, everyone filed out of the room leaving me alone with the young scholar and museum director. "I've never heard anything quite like that," Chris remarked. "It reminds me of the sound made by a bullroarer."

"What's a bullroarer?" I asked.

"A bullroarer is a sonic device used by a number of cultures in their rituals," Chris answered. "Usually it's made from a carved piece of bone or wood which is tied to the end of a piece of string and then whirled in the air. This creates a kind of humming sound that supposedly helps to induce a trance."

"I wish I knew a way to find out how these whistles were used," I declared. "I've asked Dr. Bird at the American Museum and he doesn't recall any reference to them in the literature."

"I've never come across any reference to them either, but I do have an idea," Dr. Donnan replied enthusiastically. "We have an extensive collection of photographs of Moche pottery that has been assembled in an archive here at the museum. We have nearly ten thousand slides in our collection. Moche pottery was made by the Mochica culture," Chris explained. "They were a people who inhabited the same geographic area as the Chimú, the same river valleys, but prior to the Chimú," he added.

"Dr. Bird told me about the Moche when I visited him in New York," I said, remembering the archaeologist's detailed explanation.

"I don't know if Dr. Bird mentioned it to you, but the Moche drew or painted elaborate scenes on many of their pots." Chris continued. "They also made whistle pots, though not nearly in the quantities made by later cultures. Several scholars are examining the painted scenes in order to better understand Moche culture. If you were to examine the photographs carefully, you might find one of the whistles represented. Discovering an example portrayed in the art might provide the context in which they were originally used."

"I would love to work here," I replied, scarcely believing my good fortune. "When can I begin?"

"As soon as you like," Dr. Donnan replied.

For weeks I carefully examined the photographs, studying the details in each of them. Even an obscure representation of one of the vessels would be invaluable. But I found nothing. The weeks turned into months, and still the number of photographs that remained to be examined numbered in the thousands. On occasion I would wake with a start from my reverie to find that minutes had passed while I stared into a scene drawn by an artist more than a thousand years earlier. As I looked into the distant world of this now-vanished people, I began to feel I was on the verge of entering a hidden realm. Now and then I could see beneath the surface of a scene to discern the essential meaning preserved in the two-dimensional pictographs.

As I began to study the photographs, my first thought was that the painted, stirrup-spouted pots were not a utilitarian pottery form. The spout did not lend itself to pouring or filling with liquids. Most of these pots had been discovered in graves; the great majority of them showed little or no wear. I surmised that the vessels originally served as containers for the spirit of the person with whom they were interred.

Many of the pictures painted on the pots were divided horizontally into upper and lower scenes. The lower picture often portrayed scenes from daily life, while the upper hemisphere was inhabited by fantastic half-animal, half-human figures, fruits and vegetables with human attributes, and numerous other juxtaposed shapes, equally bizarre. I concluded that the upper painted scenes were depictions of the supernatural.

One pot was painted with a maritime scene depicting a god-like creature piloting a raft piled high with pots—of the very type that I was studying—across a body of water inhabited by fantastic creatures. I imagined this to be the journey of the spirit that inhabited each pot, over a dangerous underworld, toward its destination in the realm of the dead.

Another pot revealed a reclining woman making love on the ground with a man wearing an elaborate headdress who was attended by several winged and bird-headed assistants. One assistant was holding a Moche painted vessel close to the couple's genitals. Next to the woman's head was another painted pot and a bird-headed humanoid figure. Perhaps the creatures were messengers or aides, responsible for assisting in the transference of the spirits from the pottery vessels to the potential child that might result from the sexual union that was taking place—a graphic portrayal of the process of reincarnation.

I was convinced that the Moche's pictures painted on their earthenware vessels were a symbolic language, most probably, like all ancient art, derived from a particular revelation of the Divine Principle. Scholars called these designs "iconography." In iconography, a symbol is something that stands for something else, like a code. The scholars whom I had met in the Moche archive believed that when they finally deciphered the code they would have the answer—they would have translated a language. I believed that the symbols, in addition to representing something concrete, were also precise forms drawn to evoke a hidden reality. I also believed it possible for modern people to experience the emotions or visions that had originally inspired these artistic expressions.

It was naïve of me to express this view to the other scholars. Their reaction to my enthusiastic interpretations was my first lesson in the realities of academia. I was looked upon as an eccentric who had left his farm in Pennsylvania to stare at obscure pictures in a basement room. I was not even working toward a degree, but rather to answer a question of doubtful importance to the modern world. Restraining my enthusiasm, I concluded my examination of the photographs of the Moche ceramics in silence.

I could see through the mist of centuries the meaning of many of the drawings. I arrived at my perceptions in an unorthodox manner, by intuiting or feeling—not analyzing—their content. The object of my quest remained unfulfilled, however. I did not find even a single representation of a whistling bottle in the many thousands of photographs I had examined.

The question I asked myself was, Why was there nothing rather than something? After all, these people had portrayed almost everything else in their art, from their intimate sexual practices to their metallurgical techniques. In fact, I had even found one Moche painting of a woman with a large array of pottery, apparently displayed for sale. Nearly every ceramic form in the archaeological collections was depicted among her wares. There were two exceptions: The painted, stirrup-spouted containers that I had concluded were "spirit" vessels were not portrayed, nor was there a single example of a whistling bottle.

I answered my own question, my conclusion being what I had suspected all along: The ancient whistle was an element in a sacred endeavor. The mysterious sounds were a *call* to an ineffable world. The ritual use of these instruments was of such sanctity that it could not be portrayed—not even once in a thousand years.

What you are looking for is what is looking.

—*Saint Francis of Assisi*

W ORKING ALONGSIDE ME in the Moche archive was an artist-draftsman, Patrick Finnerty, who illustrated the books and articles written by scholars in the anthropology department. During my months of study in the basement room, the laconic Irishman and I became friends. Frequently we would walk over to the coffee shop for a cup of espresso and some conversation.

One morning Patrick suggested that we go for coffee and on the way he would show me the UCLA physics library. Physics was Patrick's hobby, and my friend spent much of his time reading scientific articles and corresponding with scholars in the field. The physics library was directly across the quadrangle from Haines. Within minutes I was in a silent room on the second floor of Kinsey Hall. Intent in their study, students sat reading at rectangular wooden tables and in the few overstuffed chairs scattered throughout the room.

Thinking that perhaps I might gravitate toward some book or article of particular relevance, I walked around aimlessly, practicing a relaxed, non-focused awareness. As I wandered among the stacks, the titles of the books seemed to describe hidden realms no less enigmatic than the distant world of the Moche. "Hadrons," "Mesons," and "Quarks" were names from an equally unfamiliar dimension, and not a single volume beckoned me to reach out for it. A magazine rack with an assortment of periodicals finally drew my attention. I saw a journal with the word *acoustics* in its title, and I reached for it. As I leafed through its pages, a special insert with a glossy photograph of a man caught my eye. "For the first time in history," I read, "the silver medal in physics had been awarded to a scientist working in acoustics."

The man in the picture was Dr. Isadore Rudnick. An accompanying biography enumerated the scientist's distinguished research accomplishments. Scanning the article, I didn't notice where the physicist was employed. My almost whimsical jaunt to the UCLA specialty library, however, reminded me of the excitement and anticipation I had felt when I initiated the formal study of my whistle at the Franklin Institute. The institute's study conducted by Mr. Hargens had measured only individual instruments; my discovery of the unusual effect created by playing multiple instruments was subsequent to Mr. Hargens' report. If I could enlist the help of someone with Dr. Rudnick's expertise, perhaps the study of the whistles' unique interaction would help reveal their original purpose.

Offhandedly I asked the librarian for a copy of the UCLA phone book to find the listing for the acoustics section of the physics department. Out of curiosity, I looked up the name "Rudnick" to see if by some chance he worked at UCLA. To my wonder and delight I found Dr. Rudnick's name and his telephone number listed. This was the man I was looking for.

I had chanced upon Dr. Rudnick's picture in a national science journal without any knowledge of his existence, his importance in the field of acoustics, or his whereabouts. Yet in the space of only a few moments all those parameters had been bridged. I glowed with the feeling of conscious connection. I was beginning to recognize that a greater orchestration was guiding my life. I dialed Dr. Rudnick's number into the phone on the librarian's desk.

Within minutes of my first seeing a picture of the distinguished scientist, a voice on the other end of the line warmly announced, "Hello, this is Isadore Rudnick speaking."

"Hello, Dr. Rudnick. This is Daniel Stat," I said. "I've been studying ancient Peruvian whistles here at UCLA, and I would like to discuss with you an unusual effect they produce when they are played together. At least it's unusual to me," I added. "The artifacts were made by a number of pre-Columbian cultures over a period of several thousand years," I continued. "They have been interpreted by anthropologists as liquid containers that incorporate an amusing whistle feature that facilitates venting the vessel. When the vessels are blown, however, the combined sounds of their whistles produce an unusual sensation. This sensation has a *feeling* to it, but it's a feeling that seems to be experienced *inside* the head.

"My work is based on the premise that the vessels were intentionally pitched as instruments to produce this effect," I continued. "Perhaps the whistles were used in some sort of ritual to affect consciousness. So far I've been unable to verify my hypothesis, but if I could learn how the sounds combine to interact in their unusual manner, I might be able to develop an argument along those lines."

"Are the whistles very loud?" Dr. Rudnick asked.

"Yes, nearly as loud as a tea kettle," I answered.

"I think I know what you're asking about," the scientist replied. "It's a well-known acoustical phenomena. The sensation you've described is caused by 'auditory beats in the brain.' These beats occur when closely pitched tones are played together. The effect is due to the physiology of our hearing mechanism. It is most pronounced when the combined sounds are very loud." Dr. Rudnick paused for a moment. Then he continued on another tack, "I have a meeting this afternoon with the graduate students in my section. It would be interesting for them to see and hear your whistles. Would it be possible for you to bring them over to my office?" he asked.

Patrick and I never got to the coffee shop that day. Returning to the Moche archive, I retrieved the suitcase containing my collection of vessels, and I walked over to the new physics building not far from the museum. Dr. Rudnick greeted me in his office and ushered me into an adjoining conference room, where about a dozen graduate students soon joined us. I unpacked the artifacts and reviewed for the students my earlier telephone conversation with their mentor. The young scientists seemed fascinated by the history and age of the vessels on the table in front of them.

Dr. Rudnick blew into several of the pots, listening carefully to their sounds. Then we distributed all of the vessels to the students. Within a few moments the swirl of sound that had brought me to California filled the room. The students played for several minutes, and when the sound of the whistles stopped a lively discussion ensued. Several conversations were going on simultaneously. It was exciting for me to be there. I tried to grasp what was being discussed: combination tones, aural harmonics, non-linearity, and variations in wave patterns across the basilar membrane. Once again I felt as if I had stepped into a foreign world with its own language.

Finally the students quieted down and Dr. Rudnick explained what was happening. "The effect we've just experienced is caused by 'auditory beats' in the brain," the scientist began. "Several possible reasons may be responsible for their occurrence. Most likely, their origin is due to 'combination tones' created by the physiology of our hearing."[1]

"Can you explain that so someone without a technical background can understand it?" I asked.

"I'll try," Dr. Rudnick offered. "In some instances the ear not only interprets the sounds that we hear, but it also has the capacity to add and subtract tones from one another. In effect, our ears can make up totally new sounds—sounds that do not have a source in the outer reality. Your whistles are so closely pitched that our ears are subtracting their tones from one another. The result of this inner calculation is the perception of a low, pulsating sound known as an 'auditory beat' in the brain.

"These beat frequencies," Dr. Rudnick extrapolated, "are not only due to combination tones, but are related to periodic variations in the waveform of the overlapping vibration pattern across the basilar membrane in the ear. The overlapping waves produce a corresponding variation in the time patterns of the nerve impulse."

"I think I understand the 'combination tones,'" I interjected, "but I don't understand the rest of it."

"When you hear a sound," Dr. Rudnick explained, "you are actually perceiving a vibration of the air. The sound itself doesn't travel through the air like a paper airplane; the vibration of the air produces a movement on a membrane in the inner ear. This membrane is known as the basilar membrane, and each sound creates its own unique wave. The wave across the membrane actually looks like a wave on the surface of a body of water. A whistle that has a single pitch will always form the same wave, which in turn will trigger the same nerve impulse. Is that clear?" Dr. Rudnick asked.

"Does this mean that the nerve impulse will always be perceived as the same sound?" I asked.

"That's it," Dr. Rudnick replied. "Now we'll take it a step further. The brain does not perceive the wave as a specific sound. As each wave crosses the membrane, a particular nerve impulse is triggered, converting the wave into a specific sound. Now imagine two tones from two whistles forming two distinct waves that travel across the membrane in the ear."

"Wouldn't they trigger two distinct nerves and then be perceived as two separate sounds?" I asked.

"Ordinarily they would," Dr. Rudnick answered, "except in the case of combination tones. The sustained superimposition of two tones gives rise to an occasional slight interference of the two waves. They're jostled, if you will, changing the moment of their arrival at their trigger point. What happens is that an altogether different set of nerves is activated, sending a false signal to the brain.

"The sound that's perceived," Dr. Rudnick concluded, "is comprised of both actual sounds and sounds that are self-generated due to the structure of our hearing mechanism. The effect is enhanced when the sounds are very loud. When a number of closely pitched whistles are superimposed in this manner, the effect is multiplied by each interaction."

When I left Dr. Rudnick's office my mind was struggling to understand what had been discussed. I had learned that the unusual sounds were called "auditory beats" and they were produced by our own hearing mechanism. They were not the result of some magical mixture of the tones in the air. They were a product of human physiology and a construct of human consciousness.

The subject of auditory beats had stimulated a vast amount of discussion by scholars in the field of acoustics. So far no evidence had surfaced to suggest that the clay vessels made in Peru for millennia had been *intended* to create that effect. During the course of our discussion, I expressed to the scientists my hope of somehow being able to prove my hypothesis. As I walked back to the museum, I thought that once again destiny had opened another door. Glancing up, a quotation carved into the stone lintel above a doorway caught my eye. Attributed to the scientist Michael Faraday, the quotation read, "Nothing is too wonderful to be true."

The very next day I received a call from Steve Garrett, who introduced himself as one of Dr. Rudnick's graduate students. Steve had spoken to Dr. Rudnick and received permission to study the ancient whistles in the acoustics lab. If I were willing, we would collaborate and Dr. Rudnick would oversee our work. I felt elated. It seemed as if the whistles were orchestrating their own rediscovery and, in the process, were taking me along on their journey.

Steve and I planned an approach that might give us an answer to the question I had raised. Collecting a large sample of artifacts would give us a significant number of data points. A statistical analysis of the sounds might determine if the sound of the whistles had been consciously planned. We would measure several characteristics of each instrument, correlate the data, and present our findings at a meeting of the acoustical society. Then we would write a paper that would detail our research and submit it for publication in one of the professional journals. Obtaining the vessels would be my responsibility.

I combed the art galleries in Los Angeles for information about private collections of pre-Columbian Peruvian ceramics. My association with the UCLA museum was invaluable in getting what was normally considered privileged information from art dealers, so I was able to seek out collectors.

I met a retired geophysicist who raised rare orchids and collected pre-Columbian art. (The spry gentleman showed me first an orchid that had been named for him, then a cluster of carnivorous flowers.) The man's collection of ancient pottery was extensive. In the late 1930s, when he began to collect, "you could bring back trunk loads of the 'stuff' then," he told me. "Mexico did not prohibit the exportation of pre-Columbian art. My wife and I drove around the country in an old Ford station wagon, buying pots and figurines in village markets."

Another collector was a business leader, head of a huge, multinational corporation. The man invited me to his home to have dinner with his family. Afterward I played a game of billiards with one of his sons, and then the industrialist showed me his pre-Columbian art. Dramatically displayed on glass shelves behind sliding glass doors, the ceramics had an almost contemporary feel. Here and there an ancient textile or brightly colored feather painting provided a textural and color contrast to the modeled pottery and clay figurines. The man told me he had been attracted to the art years earlier, when he had worked in Peru. The industrialist had made the most of the earlier political situation and had assembled most of his collection while on assignment in South America.

I explained to everyone I met that I hoped the acoustical analysis would reveal an intelligible pattern to the ancient sounds. If we could determine that the whistles were intentionally pitched, I argued, then my hypothesis that they had been employed as mind-altering instruments was tenable. Most important, if we could reconstruct the old technology, we might be able to enter an altogether different reality, a reality first discovered and explored by the pre-Columbian Andean people, but that had lain dormant for centuries.

Even in Southern California, with its supermarket approach to the strange and bizarre, my research was considered "far out." Without exception, everyone I approached was intrigued with the idea that the Incas might have used the whistles as a doorway to another dimension. I was able to borrow every vessel I could locate. Occasionally I would purchase or trade for one that produced a markedly clear and resonant tone. In this way, I added to my own collection and assembled what I began to view as a "tuned" set of instruments. The thought that a specific combination or number of whistles might eventually clarify their original intent was exciting; it fueled my desire to obtain more.

In the midst of the lab work, another marvelous synchronicity occurred. It happened on the day I had arranged to measure the whistles from the collection of the California business leader, who insisted on personally delivering his artifacts to me in the lab. The collector arrived in a chauffeured limousine, dressed in a blue pinstriped suit, white shirt, and necktie. While the industrialist and his chauffeur carted the carefully wrapped pottery up the stairs to the lab on the second floor of the physics building, my father arrived on campus for his one and only visit to see me at UCLA. I imagined my father, a pragmatic businessman, was a bit puzzled by my desire to pursue research that had little or no economic consequence. I don't know what he expected to see in the physics lab ... perhaps a couple of students conducting an experiment with test tubes bubbling over a Bunsen burner, or, insofar as it was an acoustics lab, analyzing the sounds of a tuning fork.

Instead my father met the president of a Fortune 500 company who was personally involved in my research. Better yet, the industrialist suggested that the two men walk through the UCLA sculpture garden while Steve and I measured his whistles. I don't know what they talked about, but when the men returned to the lab, I could tell my father had a different idea about what I was doing.

Preliminary measurements determined that many of the whistles produced up to seven harmonic partials or overtones of the basic or fundamental frequency. I learned that when the whistles are played together the overtones also interact with each other, creating subtle harmonies that undoubtedly enhance the overall effect. This interaction of overtones creates a sound that has a correlate to a type of unique, Buddhist chant recited by specially trained Tibetan lamas.

The ethno-musicologist, Houston Smith, describes the phenomena of the lamas' chants as having no referents to ordinary experience. The sounds evoke profound feelings of adoration and awe, and integrate deep, human concerns into the lamas' prayers. Smith suggests that the lamas' chants are evocative of these feelings because they are *rich in overtones.* Sensed without being explicitly heard, overtones awaken numinous feelings because they parallel in man's hearing the relation in which the sacred stands to his life. They are a hint of something *more;* something that can be sensed but not seen; something that can be heard, but not discerned explicitly.[2]

During the process of collecting artifacts for our study, I noticed that whistles from some cultures seemed to produce entirely different tones than whistles made by other cultures. Chimú and Inca vessels, for instance, were noticeably higher in pitch than whistles made by the earlier cultures, such as the Vicus or Chancay. Also, a number of vessels (primarily from four of the earliest cultures—Salinar, Vicus, Gallinazo, and Moche) produced two notes, not simultaneously but in succession, as the breath diminished. The second note was much lower than the first and would last only for a few seconds at the very tail end of the breath. This change in pitch produced a haunting effect reminiscent of the call of a loon at twilight. It was an eerie sound, and I imagined it being used to evoke a spirit.

One evening I visited a collector who owned several examples of both Vicus and Chancay whistling vessels. The Vicus and Chancay were different Andean cultures that existed centuries apart in time and in separate geographic locales. The collector and I played two Chancay vessels and then two vessels made by the Vicus. I was excited to discover that both pairs of instruments produced the distinctive sensation that Dr. Rudnick had identified as auditory beats in the brain. Playing a Vicus and a Chancay whistle together did not create the unusual auditory effect. It appeared that the two cultures were trying to effect the same acoustical phenomena, but within a different frequency range.

The acoustical measurements in the lab all but confirmed it. Steven Garrett and I measured seventy-three whistles made by nine pre-Columbian cultures and discovered that they grouped acoustically by culture. The earlier cultures tended to pitch their whistles in the lowest range, while later cultures made whistles of a higher pitch. Gallinazo, Vicus, and Moche whistles were pitched in the 1200–1300-cycle frequency range. Chancay and Recuay whistles were pitched in the 2000–2100-cycle range. Chimú and Inca whistles averaged 2600–2800 cycles. Either this was a wonderful coincidence arising from some occult morphology within the molded shapes, or the whistles had been pitched with intention. I could not imagine that the makers of these pots had tuned them with anything less than careful attention. With the publication of our article detailing Steve's and my research, I felt in some measure vindicated.[3]

Although the original purpose for the ancient pottery whistles remained unknown, real science now had a published report confirming my hypothesis. Unlike my failure with the mining company, I had finally accomplished something of substance. Although I was not an official member of the academy, I was deeply comforted in my belief that I had found a community where I was welcome to pursue my dream.

Like the Druzes, like the moon, like death, like next week, the distant past forms part of those things that can be enriched by ignorance.

—*Jorge Luis Borges*

A T THIS POINT MY LIFE AND MY WORK were inseparable. Totally preoccupied with unraveling the mystery of the whistles, I shared my story with everyone I met and demonstrated the unusual effect of the sounds whenever I had an opportunity to do so. I wasn't just a man with a mission, I had *become* that mission. As word spread about my work, I began to receive invitations from avant-garde psychotherapists and a variety of spiritual communities and New Age centers to speak about and demonstrate the unique effect I had rediscovered.

In May 1976, I drove north from Los Angeles on the Pacific Coast Highway toward Esalen Institute in Big Sur. Dr. Stanislav Grof, Esalen's resident scholar, had invited me to participate in his month-long workshop, "Schizophrenia and the Visionary Mind." In preparation, I had read Dr. Grof's pioneering book *Realms of the Human Unconscious: Observations from LSD Research.*[1] I was excited by the opportunity to visit the renowned New Age center. The illustrious psychiatrist's workshop was exactly the sort of venue I had hoped to find for my whistles. In some manner, I felt I had arrived.

About thirty miles north of San Luis Obispo, the Pacific Coast Highway begins to undulate as it follows a series of mountain spurs that jut out into the ocean. Below the highway, the surf crashes against mammoth, seaweed-covered boulders that look like prehistoric creatures emerging from the sea. Perched on this primordial and dramatic coastline, Esalen was perhaps the best known of the California centers that had arisen in response to the burgeoning interest in deepening or expanding human awareness.

Early in the twentieth century, Big Sur had been designated a national park. With the completion of the Pacific Coast Highway, a never-ending stream of sightseers had been drawn to the dramatic plunge of mountainous coastline. Esalen was a few miles south of the park, on a wooded hillside where a mineral spring flowed out of the mountain. Since ancient times the earth-heated water had been considered medicinal by the Indians who inhabited the area. With a modern bathhouse poised on a cliff that overlooked the ocean, Esalen Institute had evolved in modern times as a place where people from various fields of consciousness exploration could present their ideas to others. The springs that had drawn the ancient peoples for healing now served as a wellspring for New Age ideas.

May had brought a carpet of flowers to the hillsides. Wondrous clouds of monarch butterflies floated in the fragrant air. On the Esalen lawn a special tree had bloomed with great clumps of orange flowers identical in color to the butterflies. Hundreds of the winged creatures, like flowers that had separated from the tree, hovered in the air above it. It appeared as if a second tier of colored blooms had blossomed in the sky. The scintillation of orange was truly magical; it epitomized the exquisite perfection of life that inhabited the little stretch of coast on either side of the famous hot spring. Sea lions frolicked in the surf below the dramatic cliffs, and birds soared on the ocean breeze. Inextricably woven throughout this idyllic vision, a delicate yet tenacious aura of peace and balance reigned.

I brought with me a dozen of the whistling pots (many of them on loan to me for the acoustical analysis) and a slide presentation I had assembled from the Moche archive. I saw myself as some sort of New Age magician. My bag of tricks included dramatic pictures of Inca ruins as well as the mind-altering instruments used by the evolved civilization of the Andes. The whistling pots would provide a live demonstration of my theory that the people who had constructed their stone-sculpted temple cities on nearly inaccessible mountaintops had also employed highly complex sounds to enter mysterious realms.

Dr. Grof greeted me when I reached the main lodge. For nearly three weeks the pioneering psychotherapist had been providing a framework for workshop participants to explore how some psychological disorders (such as schizophrenia) might be natural processes and an opportunity for personal growth. I told Stan that this sounded very much like the ideas advanced by the Association for Transpersonal Psychology, and that my initial article on the whistles had been published in their journal. Dr. Grof informed me that he was very active with the Transpersonal Association and knew Anthony Sutich quite well. I had another glimpse of the web of connections that the whistles were opening for me.

I learned that the various techniques presented by the workshop faculty had facilitated the expression of deep feelings by members of the group. The participants had grown closer together as a band of intimate explorers venturing into an inner world. Dr. Grof was excited by the idea that the diversity of techniques presented in the month-long seminar had been such a powerful instrument for transformation and growth. From his perspective, it seemed a timely moment for everyone to experience the Peruvian whistles.

In the weeks preceding the workshop, I had formulated a plan for group participation. I did not want to be just another visitor, giving a talk and then departing. I hoped to weave my story into the evolving fabric of group experience. The Inca cosmology and ancient whistles would be but additional threads drawn through a complex tapestry. I hoped that my transmission would blend into the overall design, becoming another touchstone for deepening awareness.

Just outside of the Esalen building known as "The Big House," I found some dead branches that had fallen from the tall pines growing there. Tenaciously holding to the very edge of the cliff-side precipice, the trees' roots appeared to be keeping the shoreline from falling into the sea. I brought an armload of kindling into the Cape Cod-style house and arranged it in the fireplace in the large meeting room where I would be making my presentation later that evening. As I placed each stick on the hearth, I thought about the trees that had provided this fuel. The dead branches embodied both the sunny and rainy days of the past, when they had swayed gently in the Pacific breeze. I envisioned the fire casting a warm light in the room, igniting the subtle presence of time measured by light and decay.

Enough daylight remained for me to climb down the steep, narrow staircase to the rocky beach below the house. Giant boulders at the base of the cliff formed a shoreline reef that protected the softer earth from the relentless movement of the tides. Taking off my clothes, I made my way over the rough rocks to the water. Then I edged my way down the side of a boulder and lowered myself into the bracingly cold Pacific current. Taking a deep breath, I submerged my whole body beneath an incoming wave. The sea was tumultuous: a pounding, seething force, pushing and pulling me against the rocks. When I surfaced, I shouted in exhilaration. As I climbed back up the cliff toward the house, I felt the ocean had energized me for the evening's presentation.

By eight o'clock everyone had assembled in the large meeting room. With my back to the fire and my collection of artifacts on the rug in front of me, I began to speak. The soft glow of flickering light illuminated the old vessels, and somehow I felt supported by this cast of pre-Columbian characters.

"I'm very grateful to be here," I began, looking into the faces of the couple of dozen people sitting with me on the carpeted floor. "As you know, I'm here tonight to share these instruments with you. I'm also here to share an experience that has had a profound impact on my life." Picking up the vessel that had initiated my journey, I continued, "Four years ago I bought this vessel at an auction in Pennsylvania. It was made nearly a thousand years ago in Peru. Somehow, it has survived the centuries. Through vicissitudes of great time and distance it has made its way to this place and to this evening." I paused again for a moment and then continued.

"When I bought this, I was a collector of 'things.' I lived my life in pursuit of money and social prestige, and as an adult, I had never been touched by anyone. In retrospect, I can see now how isolated I really was. Before my experience with this vessel, I never shared my feelings with *anyone* else. In fact, I don't know if I knew what they were myself."

Quietly I continued, "One afternoon I began to play this whistle. Somehow, its sound pierced the shell of a life in which I had encapsulated myself. I saw the lies and the shallowness. I saw how selfish I had become, and I was ashamed. What I saw gave me the imperative to begin again. Outwardly my new direction has been the search to find the original purpose of this instrument. But inwardly I have also been searching ... searching for an understanding of who I am to answer the question: *Why* am I here? Although I have been invited to Esalen to share my discovery with you," I affirmed, looking down at the silent crowd of clay figurines on the rug in front of me, "I am *really* here to share myself."

I paused and another minute or so went by, accented only by the sounds of the fire and the distant surf. The silence was without strain, and it seemed as if the warmth of the group deepened and reached out to include me. Then I resumed my presentation. "Before driving up to Esalen I came upon a story about a Zen artist. I want to share that story with you.

"The king of the country in which the artist lived heard of the man's marvelous artistic ability and asked him to paint a picture in a room of the king's castle. The artist agreed, on the condition that neither the king nor anyone else would enter the room until the painting was completed. The king agreed to the artist's request. Years went by until finally the king was very old. Still he had not seen the painting. One day, fearful he might soon die, he summoned the Zen master and asked if he might see the painting.

"The master replied it was indeed completed, and so the king eagerly entered the room. There, covering an entire wall, was the most wondrous landscape the king had ever seen. For many minutes he said nothing. The aged monarch was completely absorbed by the realism of the scene in front of him. Finally the king exclaimed how truly wonderful it was, well worth waiting for. The artist replied that the painting actually had been finished some years before, but his patron had not been ready to see it until then.

"Pointing to a road that disappeared into the landscape, the king asked, 'Where does that road lead?' 'I don't know,' replied the artist. 'If you wait here I will go and find out.' With that, the Zen master turned and walked into the painting. Within a few moments he disappeared behind the first hill. The king waited and waited, but the artist never returned." As I finished the story, the subdued crackle of the fire and the ocean breeze against the wood frame house were the only sounds left in the room.

"I'm not trying to compare myself to a Zen master," I said, "but I think it's important for you to immerse yourself in the experience we're going to have here tonight. This is not a demonstration of another meditation technique, but a participation in an unknown art. To the extent that you allow yourself to 'walk into the painting,' the more of the picture you will be able to see."

A slight stir indicated readiness as people shifted into more comfortable positions on the huge pillows that served as the only furniture in the room. "I've brought some slides that portray the country and the archaeological ruins of the people who made these instruments," I continued. "I think they'll give more of a context to the experience of playing the whistles." In an instant the modern magic of a tape player and a slide projector brought to life the sound and color of South America. A cheerful tune played through a reed flute brought the music of Peru into the room. A breathtaking view of the Andes Cordillera filled a large screen that had been pulled down from the ceiling like an old-fashioned window shade.

For the next thirty minutes everyone watched the slides I had selected from the nearly ten thousand that comprised the Moche archive. Every few seconds the frame changed to reveal another aspect of life or an artifact from pre-Columbian times. Interspersed with photographs of textiles, metal sculptures, and pottery were stunning views of Inca ruins, set like jewels into the rugged mountainsides. Each picture conveyed an architectural perspective of delicate balance and subtle harmony, a vivid presentation of the mastery achieved by the Andean builders. Silently the workshop participants watched the projected scenes while the eyes of the modeled clay figurines on the carpeted floor stared into space.

Chan-Chan's adobe ruins flashed into view, its once towering walls slowly eroding in the rainless decades and mild winds of the Peruvian north-coast climate. "This is the capital city of the people who made these *very* instruments," I declared, gesturing toward the crowd of artifacts sitting with me on the rug. The dancing shadows of firelight were animating the expressions on the modeled faces of the old figurines. Contrasted with Chan-Chan, the abandoned and forlorn capital city of the Chimú, the earthenware figures became a transmission across centuries, a legacy left by one people for another.

A dazzling picture of a golden object set with turquoise and jade prompted me to comment, "That is an ear spool worn exclusively by members of the ruling class. The Spanish conquerors identified members of the Inca family through this apparent badge of nobility. They called the men who wore them *orjones,* or 'big ears.' To consolidate their rule, the Spanish soldiers killed or enslaved anyone found wearing the disks.

"A coming-of-age ceremony took place at the spring equinox," I continued. "It was a graduation or knighthood rite for the young men who completed the education afforded the nobility. During the final act of that ceremony, the supreme Inca pierced the earlobes of each candidate.

"This Andean practice corresponds to acupuncture," I continued. "The Chinese identify the point where the Incas pierced the earlobe as being connected to the eye. It's interesting that, independent of the Oriental system, European physicians in the early part of this century treated myopia and cataracts by piercing the earlobe at that point and inserting a gold or silver pin. On the ancient Chinese map of the acupuncture meridians, *that* point is referred to as 'the cosmic receptivity zone.'"

The last picture in my presentation showed a sunset off the north coast of Peru near the Moche Valley. In the foreground was a ship, wrecked in shallow Pacific waters. In the center was a seagull in flight, one wingtip seeming to touch the radiant orange globe of the setting sun. It was an exquisite photograph, taken in the early 1960s by a Peace Corps volunteer who worked in Peru. Somehow the ship represented to me the iron technology and might brought to the New World by the Spanish conquerors, while the bird touching the sun represented the fate of a once-free people. Time froze that moment as a pictograph of the archetypal New World quest.

Picking up one of the artifacts, I resumed my presentation. First I related the Andean myth of Creation and how I drew upon that in my understanding of the earthenware whistles. Then I began to speak about my research into the acoustics of the vessels. "My work at UCLA strongly suggests that these vessels were pitched within a specific frequency range. Until now they have been interpreted by anthropologists as amusing liquid containers. I believe the only thing they ever contained were the breaths of the people who once played them. After tonight, they will contain your breaths as well.

"Occultists across the ages have taught that air contains an esoteric substance or principle from which all activity, all vitality, all of life is derived. The ancient wisdom traditions maintain that this vital force is brought into the body with the breath. One prominent example of this lies within the Hindu tradition. In Sanskrit, the word for 'breath' is *prana,* which signifies the energizing life principle in constant pulse with the environment. The word *prana* actually means 'absolute energy,' and refers to the potential that Yogis consciously direct, through their science of breath control, to heal or energize themselves. Breathing techniques enable adepts to store this *prana* in the brain, and the powers attributed to advanced occultists are due mainly to their knowledge and conscious use of this essential substance.

"Playing these instruments requires an attentive direction of your breath. To achieve the note designed into each of these vessels, focus your awareness on your breath. Listening to the sound of the whistle may enable you to hear subtle changes in your breathing. You can also monitor the smoothness and amplitude of your whistle and adjust your blowing pressure accordingly."

I distributed the artifacts, asking those with instruments to form a circle in the middle of the room and the others to sit as close to the circle as they could comfortably get. Taking a deep breath, I blew into the vessel that I was still holding in my hands. It was the whistle pot I had bought at the auction in Pennsylvania, seemingly a lifetime ago. The full, penetrating sound of the whistle filled the room, sustained by my breath for perhaps half a minute. As my exhalation expired, the note gradually diminished until the last air in my lungs passed through the ancient instrument as a whisper.

After a long moment I spoke to a man sitting directly across from me in the circle. "Try playing a note." With more force than was necessary, the man blew his breath into the artifact. The sound rose quickly to its designed pitch and volume, then the sound ended in a sputter. Only the forced *whoosh* of the man's breath could be heard emanating from the clay vessel.

"Take another breath. This time blow into it more softly," I suggested. "Relax. We have plenty of time. As you play, *listen* to the sound of the whistle. Hear it as a reflection of your inner energy flowing into the outer world."

The man inhaled deeply. Then, with awareness, he blew his breath into the ancient artifact. This time his breath was transformed into the full, piercing sound of the instrument. Reaching maximum volume, he controlled the force of his exhalation, sustaining the note until it smoothly trailed off into silence.

"That's the first time I ever listened to my breath," he observed. "The sound of the whistle really gives you a chance to hear it. Perhaps these instruments were used to teach people breathing techniques, something like the yogic practices you mentioned."

One by one, each person in the circle played a note on their vessel. Some needed several attempts before they could discern the amount of pressure they needed to exert. Within a few minutes everyone had mastered his or her instrument. Then I asked three people holding vessels to play six breaths together.

"Try to be aware of the other whistles as well as your own," I instructed. "Some of these whistles are a little louder than others, but you can modulate your note to play along with the rest of the group. Be sensitive to the overall volume. The tones interact in a special way, but the effect will vary depending on everyone's sensitivity.

"The other thing to remember is that, although we'll all begin together, each of us has a distinctive breathing pattern and lung capacity. Be as comfortable as possible. Don't try to sustain your note any longer than you would if you were playing alone, and don't stop playing before you would naturally, even if everyone else has stopped. When you reach the end of a breath, pause for as long as you'd like—until you're comfortable—before taking your next breath. Being true to yourself, as far as playing or not playing your one note is concerned, is the most you can add to the overall orchestration of these instruments."

Within seconds the otherworldly wail of phantom tones seemed to saturate the room with sound. By the second or third breath the group had intuited their interaction, and each person was aware of her ability to weave a single note into the complex tapestry of sound. The unexpected and pervasive effect produced by the combined whistles created a stir among the rest of the group. The initial reaction was one of surprise, soon followed by curiosity as to what was happening. When the sounds finally stopped, someone exclaimed, "Did anyone else hear *that?* I could 'feel' the sounds *inside* my head!"

"I don't know exactly how these sounds affect the mind," I said. "But I do have a theory as to why the whole experience leaves people feeling centered afterward. I think it has to do with the tremendous effort the brain makes to *locate* the sounds that we describe as having a 'feeling.' The sound we feel is an inner production. The sound itself does not have a location in space, in the outer reality, and therefore it cannot be processed in the usual way we process and locate other sounds. In effect, the combined sounds of the whistles create a self-imposed barrier that prevents us from achieving a balanced reality. At the end of five or ten minutes of creating for ourselves this intense mental activity—trying to find and organize sounds that don't exist—a moment finally arrives when the chaos ends and the disequilibrium we ourselves have created is resolved.

"Any slight disharmony to which we've learned to adjust may be overcome by the extraordinary mental effort expended to regain a structured world. It's comparable to pushing against an obstacle with your hand for a few minutes. When the barrier is finally removed, the muscles no longer have anything to resist, and any minor obstruction is easily pushed aside. The same may be true for the mind. The sheer force of the brain's sustained effort to achieve a harmonious structure, a balanced reality, may overwhelm whatever mental obstruction we've learned to live with.

"The effect may be similar to a Zen koan," I added. "A Zen koan is a mental puzzle, an unanswerable question given by a Zen Buddhist master to his disciple, designed to frustrate the student's mind. The idea is that the ego or personality will finally disappear when it reaches a state of absolute frustration. All of the techniques devised by the various spiritual traditions are designed to somehow still the mind. If the whistles are part of a lost spiritual tradition, then they may have been designed to accomplish the same purpose."

I asked the first three people to begin playing again and indicated the order in which the others with instruments should join in. "This time, play for as long as you wish," I instructed. "If you feel you want to stop playing and listen, then do so, regardless of when you feel like stopping. Later, if you're so inclined, rejoin the group, even if it seems that everyone else is finished and only one or two whistles are being played. The only thing to remember is to be true to yourself."

The three people I had chosen began to play together and were joined one at a time by the others. Within a few minutes, the dozen instruments were creating a barrage of tones that seemed to emanate from all the surfaces in the room. No one could escape the powerful acoustical phenomena. A few people appeared to brace themselves for the onslaught, to somehow resist the exotic and unknown force. It was impossible to resist, however. The sounds were an inner production. We could not define the sounds' outer reality or structure our environment in the ordinary manner.

Several people stretched out on the rug and, closing their eyes, surrendered to the complex harmony. One person struggled for a minute or two and, finding the effect impossible to endure, left the room. The group continued to play the ensemble of whistles for nearly an hour. At times, only one or two people were left playing, and it seemed as if the sound would momentarily stop. Then someone else would join in, and then another and another, until once again most of the whistles were being played.

The group explored every possible combination. Duets, trios, and quartets arose, harmonized for a few minutes or longer, and then dissolved into another combination. At times the whistles were soft; at other times they were loud, saturating the room with their pervasive effect. At last, a single note trailed off into silence, and an atmosphere of tranquility and warmth enveloped the group. The silence in the room was deep and palpable, embracing everyone. It was evident that even a single word would be superfluous.

After about five minutes of silence, I closed the ceremony by saying in a quiet voice, "Thank you. Thank you for inviting me here." Then people began to share how deeply touched they had been by the experience. Tears flowed from many eyes. People spoke softly and earnestly about how their hearts had opened, and how they felt imbued with love, gratitude, awe, and beauty. I felt this, too, overflowing with the love of the whole Creation.

One man reported having seen a "column of light" that pierced the ceiling and floor of the room. "From within the column, iridescent swirls of energy radiated out into all of us. It was beautiful," he said, and then added, "I will *never* be the same."

A young woman reported a man's face had appeared to her. She told us, "He was wearing a diaphanous, woven veil—thin, like a spider's web—that encompassed his head and covered his face." The veil was so delicate she could see the man's features. "He seemed to have come from another time," she told us. "He looked deeply into my eyes, in acknowledgment and support of my Being." Others reported seeing birds and angels, hearing the whisper of spirits that spoke in strange tongues, and hearing the *anahata* or unstruck sound that emanates from the underlying reality of Creation.

Despite my initial journey of light that had propelled me into a new life, I could never have imagined the outcome of playing my whistles with these people. I wanted the evening never to end. I wanted to make these people my family. My heart ached to live my life co-creating with people like this. I wished to live with the depth of feeling I had shared with the others. For the first time in my life, I felt visible. I had never imagined this possible. I didn't even know it existed or that I missed it. To open my heart in this manner was what I had been searching for.

$E = mc^2$

—*Albert Einstein*

Even though you tie
a hundred knots—the
string remains one.

—*Rumi*

FOLLOWING DR. GROF'S WORKSHOP I stayed on at Esalen for a few days. One morning at breakfast I met a group of physicists who had gathered at the retreat center to share their ideas and discuss their work. They included Saul-Paul Sirag and Nick Herbert, as well as Jeffrey Mishlove, Alan Wolf, and Gary Zukav. The conversation that morning was wide-ranging and resembled in some aspects the discussions of the physicists back at UCLA. I noted a difference, however. In addition to the scientific and technical jargon that I had grown accustomed to hearing in the acoustics lab, these men seemed to bring a flavor of Eastern metaphysics into the conversation. The word *consciousness* kept creeping into the discussion.

I told the men about my work with the ancient whistles and my journey of discovery that had brought me to Esalen. The young scientists were intrigued and eager to experience the effect for themselves. I retrieved the suitcase that contained my whistles, and a group of us walked down the few steps from the deck at the Esalen lodge to a small lawn nearby. We sat in a circle on the grass. Six or seven of the men began to play while the rest of us listened. The swirl of sound rose into the air. To my ears it sounded as if a chorus of cicadas had arrived on the Esalen lawn.

After everyone had stopped playing, a few minutes of silence ensued. Then a discussion began about difference tones, binaural beats, and the possibility that the sounds in some way synchronized the electrical activity between the hemispheres of the brain. Saul-Paul made a comment about a Frequency Following Response, and theorized that perhaps electrical "entrainment" due to an FFR was the mechanism that enabled hemispheric synchronization to take place.

I'd first heard about a Frequency Following Response from Mr. Hargens at the Franklin Institute. The idea it might play a part in the physiology of our response to the ancient sounds piqued my interest.

"Can you elaborate on that?" I asked the young physicist.

"During ordinary, waking consciousness, electrical activity in the brain can be measured in most people at around thirty cycles per second." Saul-Paul explained. "This is known as a 'Beta' state of consciousness. It is possible, though, to change the brain's electrical activity by presenting a person with a strong, sustained pulse of sound or light of a different frequency. This can take place, however, only within certain limited parameters. If the stimulus continues for a sustained period of time, the brain's electrical activity may initially be 'nudged' by it, then 'entrained' to the frequency of the stimulus.

"For example, a meditative or 'Alpha' brainwave state may be induced by entraining the brain's electrical activity to a tone pulsing at eight to twelve cycles per second. This corresponds to the brainwave activity that experienced meditators or Yogi adepts achieve through meditation or while in deep contemplation. Slowing down the brainwaves even further, to three and a half to seven cycles per second, will produce what is called the 'Theta' state. Sleep researchers have discovered this range of brainwave frequency occurs when a person is dreaming. According to some theorists this frequency is also generated when a person has a visionary experience.

"Finally, the slowest measurable brainwave state is when the frequency of the brain's electrical activity slows to the 'Delta' state. In Delta, the brain's electrical waves pulse between one and three cycles per second. This corresponds to the brain's activity when a person is in a very deep sleep, deeper even than the Theta or dream state. It's been theorized that this is when the body rejuvenates itself and self-healing takes place.

"The difference tones or beat frequencies produced by the whistles may correspond to one or another of these other-than-waking brainwave states," Saul-Paul concluded. "If that's the case, then brainwave entrainment might be the mechanism through which an altered state of consciousness is induced.

Finally I posed a question that had been lingering in my mind since breakfast: "How does consciousness relate to physics?" Jeffrey Mishlove, a Ph.D. candidate in parapsychology from the University of California at Berkeley and a radio talk-show personality in San Francisco, responded, "A new direction in physics takes a traditional scientific approach but also accounts for current research into the nature of consciousness. In the past, mechanistic science defined human beings as essentially biological machines; consciousness was viewed as a product of the physiological processes in the brain. Now some physicists are beginning to think the mind is an active and crucial attribute of existence—all existence, not just man's existence. It's what mystics have been saying all along."

"The new view postulates that consciousness may not be unique to biological creatures," Saul-Paul added. "Consciousness may be a universal phenomenon. The reason modern physics is struggling to reach a new paradigm is that Newton's clear separation between matter and space does not always exist. Observations in sub-atomic physics have encountered a series of paradoxes, especially in the study of light. What's been discovered is that there is no clear separation between matter and space. In the new model, space is viewed as a web of energy that contains the potential to create matter."

"How does this tie in with mysticism? " I questioned.

"Mystics maintain that all is one. Differences are merely different manifestations of the same ultimate reality," Saul-Paul answered. "Mystery schools teach the universe is a whole, interdependent, and interconnected web, a 'living' reality conscious of itself. Only man's mind divides the world, which leads us to experience ourselves as isolated, individual selves. Now the physicist, the arch-scientist, who has been dividing and quantifying, exploiting the separatist view to the extreme, is seeing evidence of the mystical truth in his laboratory and is seriously questioning his earlier beliefs."

"Not long ago I had a conversation with the archaeologist, Junius Bird," I interjected. "Dr. Bird told me about a cosmology held by the Incas and other pre-Columbian cultures who lived in South America. Those people viewed the entire material world as being connected through a 'spirit' that pervades the universe. Perhaps what modern man is discovering is what ancient people knew all along."

After the physicists had dispersed I sat on a wooden bench at the edge of the cliff overlooking the ocean. Sparkles of sunlight flickered in the water as the tide gently surged back and forth.

Although playing the whistles with the scientists had not evoked the same feelings I had felt with the workshop participants, the men's conversation and curiosity about how the world works added another dimension to life.

I was sitting on the western edge of the continent. I had traveled very far from my former life on the east coast. My interests then had revolved around getting ahead in the world, making money, and networking with people who could further my ambitions. Rarely had I paused in my headlong rush to take time to relax and enjoy the simple beauty of the world around me. The old Chimú whistle had given me pause, though, turning me and then propelling me on a path into an unknown and unimaginable future.

When I first encountered that horrible darkness, I didn't know whether or not I could survive. But I did survive. Even more, I thrived and discovered through my work a vitality previously unknown. I was happy to be alive, and I was living a meaningful life. I was excited by my quest. My journey with the whistle had carried me into a great beauty I had never imagined. I felt satisfied in two important aspects of my life: a continuing curiosity about my discovery, and the opening of my heart to deep feelings.

I continued to watch the sparkle of sunlight on the water. I noticed the vibrant orange blossoms on the butterfly tree; a few of the monarchs hovered in the perfumed air above me. The striking color of the insect's wings shone in the sunlight. I imagined their fluttering to be another variation of the light sparkles dancing on the water. A sea lion was swimming in the surf below the cliff; the creature's sleek, brown fur glistened like dark velvet. My eyes rested on a cool, translucent green frond of seaweed undulating in the surf. I wondered if the scientists' thoughts were another scintillation like sunlight: electrons dancing in the physicists' minds. Sitting on the wooden bench at Esalen, I could feel the warmth from the sun on my skin . . . yet another glimmer of the same light.

In the spiritual world there are no time divisions such as the past, present and future, for they have contracted themselves into a single moment where life quivers in its true sense.

—*D. T. Suzuki*

PERHAPS NOWHERE ELSE in the Western Hemisphere was the winter solstice as celebrated as it was in Berkeley, California, during 1975. All day Saturday, Saturday night, and for the nearly four hours on Sunday morning before the solstice, KPFA, the Bay Area's public broadcasting station, hosted the celebration. A parade of participants, anxious to contribute their special perspective on the solstice, took turns at the microphone during the marathon program. Berkeley was perhaps uniquely qualified as the American city best able to attract the widest variety of perspectives. Everyone was there, from the Anchorites to the Zoroastrians.

I carried the Peruvian whistles into the studio in a yellow suitcase. After checking in with one of the program coordinators, I learned I was scheduled to go on the air Saturday morning and then make another presentation sometime before the moment of solstice at about 4:00 A.M. It was a long day, but the intriguing stream of people who filtered in and out of the building during the broadcast condensed the time into what later would seem only a few hours, and later still but a brief moment.

In anticipation of the program, I had studied the Mayan civilization with the intent that, in addition to discussing the Peruvian whistles, I would talk about ancient Mayan cosmology. The winter solstice was the beginning of the Inca year, and in pre-Columbian times it had been the most important celebration of the year. My plan was to embellish my explication of the solemn Inca ceremony with a synthesis of Mayan calendrics. I had chanced upon an important piece of information that I planned to share with the radio audience.

Like the Incas, the Mayans were a highly developed civilization that had flourished in the Yucatan area of Mexico, Guatemala, and Honduras before Columbus arrived in the New World. Most interesting, and perhaps the dominant signature of the culture, was the fact that an obsessive reckoning of calendar time orchestrated all of Mayan life. For many centuries the people had synchronized their lives with various planetary cycles. They discerned an order to the universe with which they aspired to live in concordance. Through a careful interpretation of their complex calendar, the Mayans had determined favorable days for initiating specific activities and had identified unlucky days as well. The result was a highly developed astrological-religious cosmology presided over by an extensive hierarchy of astrologer-priests.

These clergy were the people responsible for building the complex temple plazas and pyramids discovered in Palenque, Chichen Itza, and Tikal: mysterious ceremonial centers where Mayan astrologers had carefully observed the turning of the world. As I read about their civilization, I visualized the Mayan priests keeping track of the days in their complex calendar and giving advice to govern the lives of the people. My plan for the solstice broadcast was to share with the radio audience what I had gleaned from this esoteric information.

I was introduced on the air by Jeffrey Mishlove, who was serving as one of the hosts for the marathon program. Jeffrey gave a brief synopsis of my research at UCLA and my quest to discover the meaning of the ancient Peruvian whistles. Then he turned the microphone over to me.

"In Peru, the solstice is known as 'Inti-Raymi,' which means 'solemn dance of the sun,'" I declared, speaking into the microphone with a touch of melodrama in my voice. "In ancient times the movement of the sun between the solstices was viewed as a solemn dance, and the solstice ceremony was regarded as the most solemn event of the year. For a people who carefully calibrated the lateral movement of the sun where it arose on the horizon, the exact moment when the golden orb changed direction for its journey of return was the critical moment. The sun's return within its designated cycle was imperative, for upon its light depended the life of the world. Prayers and supplications by every human being were essential to help maintain the orderly change in direction, and the solstice ritual was an ultimate moment for a people who referred to themselves as 'children of the sun.'"

That was the overview. As I described the details of the Inca solstice ritual to the radio audience, I included my interpretation and understanding of the pre-Columbian whistles. "The potter who made the instruments that we are about to play here," I declared, stepping deeper into my role as counterculture anthropologist, "received the fire for his kiln during an Inti-Raymi ceremony that took place nearly a thousand years ago."

I began to integrate my understanding of Mayan calendrics into the discussion. Somewhere I had read that when Cortez first made contact with the Aztecs in 1519, he was informed that twelve years earlier, the anniversary of the fifty-two-year cycle known as the "calendar round"' had been celebrated. Extrapolating from this information, I announced that the calendar round of the Mayans (from whom the Aztecs had received their calendar) had therefore ended in 1507. A succession of fifty-two-year cycles brought the anniversary of that crucial historical event right into the present moment—the 1975 winter solstice being celebrated and broadcast live over Berkeley public radio. I was serious in my pronouncement, adopting what I imagined to be the somber manner of a Mayan priest officiating at the ritual celebration of an event that would take place but once in his adult life.

"For nearly five hundred years," I declared, "the sacred round of fifty-two-year cycles has passed unnoticed. Now we are picking up the count once again, measuring and acknowledging a very special unit of time established by a highly advanced civilization. The Mayan calendar round," I explained, "is a cycle that integrates into a single time period both the Mayan sacred year of 260 days and their solar, or 'vague' year, comprised of 365 days. Imagine two gears: one with 260 teeth and the other with 365 teeth. One gear represents the sacred year and the other gear represents the solar year; each tooth represents a single day in both calendars. If the gears were meshed with the first tooth, representing the initial day of each year lined up with one another, it would take 18,980 days (assuming that the gears move one tooth each day) before both gears would return to their starting position.

"The length of time required to achieve this intriguing calculation is the fifty-two-year cycle that the Mayans identified as their 'calendar round,'" I explained, as if somehow I had something to do with devising the ingenious calculation. "The ancient Mayans considered the anniversary of the synchronization of these two cycles to be a crucial historical moment when anything could happen, including the end of the world."

The observance of this Mayan calendric anniversary was, I imagined, as significant as the underlying basis for the Inti-Raymi ceremony. I viewed the combining of these cultural beliefs on the solstice radio program as an important moment in human awareness. I also believed this was a crucial point in actual time as well, a time previously determined and scrupulously observed by generations of Mayan priests. Someone in the radio audience asked me to explain why the Mayan sacred year was comprised of 260 days.

"No one knows for sure," I replied, "but some suppose it corresponds to the human gestation cycle. The Meso-Americans may have considered the 260-day period between conception and birth to be of such vital importance that they devised a way to integrate it into the 365-day solar calendar. The fifty-two-year calendar round is actually the length of time it takes to return to the exact cosmological position that existed at the moment of conception."

"But wouldn't that be a different moment for every person?" someone asked.

"Yes, it would be a different moment for individuals," I replied. "But there may have been an historical moment that everyone in the culture counted from collectively. We know for certain that every fifty-two years the Mayans celebrated the anniversary of their calendar round by erecting a stone monument to commemorate the event.

"The Mayans also integrated a third calendar into their calculations," I added, "the 584-day Venus cycle. The Venus cycle requires exactly 104 years to synchronize with the other two calendars. The Mayan culture-hero, Quetzalcoatl, supposedly disappeared exactly 104 years after his appearance on Earth and promised to reappear in the future, as did Viracocha, his Andean counterpart. Perhaps the Mayan calculations were predicated on that event," I theorized.

"Although the Central and South American cultures were comprised of different people, both were advanced civilizations that inhabited this continent for many centuries. Not only is it possible," I declared, "but probable that their vision of the universe had intimate correspondences."

Once again, I reiterated my earlier announcement that the synthesis of the various cultural myths brought the anniversary of the Mayan calendar round to that 1975 solstice day—by far my most adventuresome speculation. At least my previous interpretations of the pre-Columbian art were based on detailed study I had actually undertaken. These last conclusions were based on so little real information it seemed I had succumbed to the glamour of becoming a radio personality, the re-interpreter of ancient American history.

During the day I made the acquaintance of a Tibetan Buddhist, Dorje Ling, who was also a guest on the solstice program. I was curious about the ornately decorated bone trumpet the monk had brought to the station to play on the solstice program. The instrument was about twelve inches long and had a beautifully wrought silver fitting that served as a mouthpiece. A band of silver encircled the other end as well. "Please tell me about your trumpet," I asked, after we'd made our acquaintance.

"This is not a musical instrument," Dorje replied, extending the object toward me so I could examine it in more detail.

As I looked at the object more carefully I could see tiny cracks in the bone, which was yellowish-ivory in color. The trumpet appeared to be very old. "I'm gathering this is an instrument that's played on ceremonial occasions, such as the solstice," I added with a smile. I remembered the afternoon in Pennsylvania when I had listened to a recording of Buddhist chants. An occasional clash of cymbals or a blast of trumpets was included in the prayers. I imagined these as punctuation marks for the monks' chants.

"Yes, we play these instruments on special occasions," Dorje answered me.

"What sort of bone is this made from?" I asked, imagining the trumpet had been made from a walrus or whalebone, like beautifully aged scrimshaw I'd seen in museum collections.

"This particular instrument was made from a woman's thighbone," the monk answered. "That's why it's so short; men's bones are usually longer."

I was mildly stunned by Dorje's revelation. We were sitting in a couple of comfortable armchairs in a lounge at the radio station, and I was holding in my hands a human thighbone! Finally, I stammered, "Why do you—why do you play human thighbones as instruments?"

"It's not just anyone's bone," he replied, retrieving the trumpet. "This is a bone from a holy person, a monk or a nun. And not from just any monk or nun. The thighbone has to be from a person who, during his or her lifetime, was considered a person of deep and peaceful persuasion, someone who was considered holy. Our tradition teaches that after a person like that dies, their special quality—their holiness—remains in a cellular alignment within their bones. When we blow our breath through a bone such as this one, molecules of their holy substance are released into the air along with our breath. It's more than invoking their memory. Playing this instrument actually sanctifies the space, bringing the essence and special quality of a prayerful person into the present moment."

I thanked Dorje for explaining this to me. The man's explanation of why Tibetan Buddhists play human thighbone trumpets provided me with a new way to consider the ancient Peruvian whistles. All along I had regarded the old pottery as sacred instruments; after all, they were *huacas*. As with the thighbone trumpets, the whistles also carried an essence from the people to whom they had once belonged.

Mystics claim there is a special essence in the breath. I imagined molecules of that essence still resided in the clay. My original vessel depicted a man sitting peacefully with his hands clasped in front of him. The man's posture was one of repose, and the position of his hands might have indicated prayer. Perhaps the old clay portrait whistles had been intended as repositories for the breath of the person with whom the vessel had been buried. If this was so, then each time a whistle was blown a miniscule trace of the original owner's breath was released into the world. Playing the old vessels may have been a means to invoke the spirit of those people.

After my discussion with Dorje Ling I found a nearby restaurant and had a quick lunch. Then I returned to the station for the remainder of the afternoon. A short time after my return, Jeffrey Mishlove joined me in the lounge. "I enjoyed your presentation this morning," Jeff told me, as he settled down into one of the armchairs. "But I have to tell you, Daniel, I disagree with your interpretation of Mayan calendrics."

"Why is that, Jeff?" I asked. "I'm pretty sure I understand the math."

"It doesn't have to do with the math," Jeffrey replied. "My disagreement with your interpretation has to do with the way you interpret time. From my perspective, if the Mayan conception of time is relevant, and I'm not sure it is, the Meso-American calendar is only relevant from the point of view of the Mayan people themselves. I don't believe their calendar has any significance for us. Einstein demonstrated that measurements involving time are relative only to each other and to the observer taking the measurements," he added.

"Can you explain what you're saying in a way I could understand it without my having to understand Einstein's theory?" I asked.

"Perhaps an analogy will help," Jeffrey replied. "You probably know light from our sun takes about eight minutes to reach Earth.

Imagine a star billions of miles from our planet; light from that star takes many years, perhaps centuries to get here. For example, light from the North Star takes 640 years to reach the Earth, and light from the two bright stars in Orion's Belt takes 1100 and 1500 years to get here. When you look up at the sky and see those stars, it only appears they are shining simultaneously. What you are seeing is the result of different events that only appear—in your vision—to be happening at the same time; your eyes see the stars as shining simultaneously. It is only your mind that orders events into a sequence you then define as 'time.' In reality, the universe is an aggregate of non-simultaneous events.

"If you think about it," Jeffrey continued, "the North Star might not even exist anymore. It may have burned out, but its light, which has traveled for 640 years to reach a visible point in your mind, exists as the record of a day six and a half centuries ago when the North Star was shining. The perception of when something occurs—which is the ordering of events—depends on the position in space of the person observing the event. Someone on a planet in the North Star's solar system, for example, would have seen the very same light 640 years ago; in our calendar that would be sometime around the year 1335."

"Does this mean that looking out into space at the stars is actually looking backward in time?" I asked, trying to grasp what Jeffrey had just told me.

"That's it exactly," Jeffrey answered. "The distance the light traveled to get here actually determines the historical sequence of the event. Time is a useful measurement only if everyone agrees to all of the parameters. That's why the concept of Mayan calendrics is relevant only from the point of view of the ancient Mayans."

"If there were a rationale for when the Mayan priests began their count, wouldn't that logic still hold true today?" I asked, trying to salvage some relevance from my elaborate speculations.

"In terms of life on Earth, time progresses for individuals. If a rationale exists for the Mayans counting off fifty-two-year cycles, then perhaps it would hold true for us as well. But so many pieces are missing it's impossible to know what those people were counting."

Shortly before the moment of solstice, I went on the air once again. This time I limited my discussion to the Inca civilization, describing the ritual celebration of Inti-Raymi and my speculations concerning the making and playing of the old whistles. Then a small group of us played the whistles for a few minutes. Where the sounds of the archaic clay pots might travel, and who might hear them in the pre-dawn darkness of that solstice morning, I could not imagine.

Driving back to Los Angeles, I thought about my participation on the solstice program. I was chagrined for having allowed my ego to propel me toward what I imagined would be a new and important role in life. I was not destined to become the re-interpreter of ancient Mayan cosmology, nor was I destined to become a counterculture anthropologist. From here on, I decided, I would stick to my primary quest. The satisfaction I derived from studying the old whistles, traveling and sharing them with others was fulfillment enough.

Most important, though, Dorje Ling's explanation of the thighbone trumpet had brought me to a new awareness. The Buddhist monk had taught me a plausible reason for the deeper truth about the *huacas*. I had wondered why all of the old clay pots were identified in the Indians' language as *huacas*. Despite my understanding of the Indians' story of Creation, I couldn't quite imagine why all whistling vessels were regarded as sacred objects. If the old clay vessels had been repositories for the breath of the Indians' ancestors, though, it was no wonder they were regarded in that way.

When I got back to Los Angeles I went right to work. Steve Garrett and I spent time together in the acoustics lab preparing to present the results of our research at a meeting of the Acoustical Society of America. Just prior to our presentation at a national meeting of the specialty physics group, the public relations department of the UCLA School of Engineering sent out a press release to the news media announcing the results of our study. The university release stated that ancient whistling bottles made by various South American cultures were tuned to specific frequencies. The press release concluded with my speculation that the instruments were probably intended to affect consciousness.

Within a few days both the *UCLA Weekly* and the University-sponsored public relations paper, the *Clip Sheet,* ran front-page articles with pictures of the clay artifacts. Both stories included my intriguing speculations and identified me as associated with the UCLA Museum of Cultural History. I saw Dr. Donnan several times during the week, and I suspected he was unhappy with the publicity. Finally, the museum director cautioned me not to speak to any of the press. Chris voiced his concern that the story might bring unwanted publicity to the museum.

When I returned from the meeting where Steve and I had read our paper, Tom Tugent, the director of public relations at the School of Engineering, contacted us with the news that George Alexander, the science writer for the *Los Angeles Times,* had requested an interview. Carried away by this moment of attention, I disregarded Dr. Donnan's warning and welcomed the impending publicity.

The newspaperman met us in Mr. Tugent's office. Mr. Alexander listened carefully as Steve and I recounted the details of our analysis and the basis for our conclusions. We showed the science writer several of the Peruvian artifacts, and three or four of us played a few notes together to demonstrate the eerie effect. The sounds of the whistles reverberated throughout the conservatively appointed office in the School of Engineering. Mr. Alexander seemed dutifully impressed.

At the conclusion of the interview, I recounted the Andean myth of Creation. "In pre-Columbian times, the Andean people believed their Creator formed the first men out of clay and breathed life into them," I began. Holding one of the artifacts, I declared, "Surely the potter who made this vessel a thousand years ago was mindful of his own root belief. If this instrument was made for a spiritual purpose, a ritual," I concluded, "unquestionably that metaphor would have been an important element in the potter's own creative process."

"Do you think the whistles were used to get 'high'?" Mr. Alexander asked.

"I think they were employed in some spiritual ceremony to affect consciousness," I answered.

Mr. Alexander noted my conjecture and the *Times* photographer who was with him took a few photos of the artifacts and a picture of Steve blowing into one of the vessels. A few days later, Mr. Alexander's story filled the top half of page 3 in the first section of the *Los Angeles Times*.[1] Two pictures of the whistles and a photo of Steve blowing into another vessel accompanied the article. The article's headline read, "Suggested by Experiments, Ancient Whistling Bottles—A 'High' for Indians?"

Mr. Alexander's story focused on the speculation that the ancient vessels had been used in some ritual during which participants became "high" by playing the whistles. The article went on to suggest that, when combined with some hallucinogenic drug, whistle blowing would certainly result in getting high. The last two paragraphs of the paper's morning edition recapitulated a literal rendition of my religious interpretations. By the newspaper's second edition, however, my interpretation had been deleted, leaving only a small amount of real information and the provocative speculation.

Upon reading the story I instinctively knew Dr. Donnan would be perturbed, although at the time I didn't know to what degree. Due to my ambiguous position at the university, I was identified in the article as "Dan Stat of the UCLA Museum of Cultural History." With some trepidation I drove over to UCLA later that morning.

Chris ushered me into the same spacious office that had been the scene of my welcome and invitation to work at UCLA. The fair-haired scholar who headed the museum seemed particularly neat that morning in his blue blazer. I noticed some tightness around Chris's eyes, and his voice was unnaturally low. "Come on in," he said, carefully measuring each word.

"I guess you've seen this," I said, weakly waving a copy of the morning paper in the man's direction.

"I've already received at least a dozen phone calls, and I'm sure there will be more," was his terse reply. "There's no way this kind of nonsense can be defended," he declared, his voice rising appreciably.

"Chris, the reporter stretched my interpretation," I replied. "I never said the whistles were used to get 'high.' I told him a likely use for them was to affect consciousness."

"There never should have been an interview," the museum director stated emphatically, his voice returning to normal. "You should have known better than to talk to that reporter. The man is in business to sell newspapers. He will emphasize whatever part of a story will best accomplish those ends. The whole thing has gone entirely too far. I'm going to cut loose from you and from your crazy ideas. I wasn't a part of your research, and as of this moment you are not associated in any way with this museum."

"Chris, I can understand why you have to ask me to leave the museum," I replied, "but there's no reason why we can't remain friends."

"Do you realize your nonsensical speculations will be read by more people than will read all of the books and articles I'll ever write about these same cultures?" Chris answered, not seeming to hear me. "Articles based on solid, scholarly research. The one thing this episode has taught me is never to allow an unsupervised nonprofessional into my museum. I suppose the next thing you'll be saying is the whistles are a cure for some disease."

"I didn't say the whistles were used to get 'high,'" I repeated. "The work we did in the lab is valid. The vessels were definitely intended as sonic devices. You've heard them yourself. The people who made them were incredibly ingenious. How do you suppose they fit those giant stones into the wall at Sacsahuaman?"

"Levitation, obviously levitation," the museum director replied, with no attempt to hide the sarcasm in his voice. "Just because Castañeda got away with it doesn't mean we're going to lend the respectability of this university to everyone who presents us with a metaphysical hallucination. As far as I'm concerned this interview is over."

My heart sank as I handed Chris the keys to the office he had so generously provided. By ignoring my sponsor's clear instructions, I had caused my treasured inclusion in the university community to end. As I trudged out of the building, the bright world I had inhabited began to darken. I saw a way of life I had really loved slipping away. Although my theory was now widely known, I had lost something of inestimable value. I was adrift in Los Angeles with a suitcase full of old clay whistles, but without a clue as to the direction I might now take.

Within a week the syndicated version of the *Los Angeles Times* article appeared in newspapers across the country. Now, I imagined, I would hear from others in academia (or somewhere), and the new direction I was looking for with my research would emerge. Occasionally the phone did ring. Writers for both *High Times* magazine and the *National Enquirer* telephoned me to ask for an interview. These were not the calls I had hoped for. The newspaper headline had brought the wolves to my door.

Weeks passed, and I did not hear from a single person whom I would consider a serious possibility for furthering my study of the ancient vessels. On one or two occasions I drove to UCLA. Without my museum permit it was difficult to find a place to park my truck. I found the graduate students at the physics lab busy with their own experiments. Patrick met me for a cup of espresso, but it wasn't like old times. Now I was just another visitor to UCLA. I didn't have a real purpose for being there. No longer was I a legitimate member of the university community.

At home I busied myself by reading accounts of travelers who had explored Peru. I was fascinated by the culture and intrigued by the descriptions of ancient ruins. Gradually it dawned on me. I needed to make the journey for myself.

Destiny sealed in the breath of a long ago dawn;
forgotten sorrow of a flower fallen;
the Inca Roca benign and strong
his dust and blood flow now
like water through the earth.

—*Daniel K. Statnekov*

MY NIGHT FLIGHT TO LIMA arrived early in the morning. I did not leave the airport to see the modern capital of Peru, which had been founded by the Spanish. Instead I connected immediately with a second flight destined for Cuzco. As the plane lifted above the fog-enshrouded city, I remembered reading that the conquerors from Spain, against the advice of the Indians, had chosen this location for their new capital. Now the damp fogs and almost daily drizzle provided a perpetual torment to Lima's inhabitants. Unfortunately it wasn't just the conquerors' descendents who suffered from the poor choice of their ancestors. Millions of Indians, seeking relief from the poverty of the provinces, suffered from the dreadful climate as well.

In contrast, the Incas had been sensitive to the effect of climate on their citizens' well-being. In the course of administering their empire, they sometimes had occasion to move entire villages from one part of their kingdom to another. They often did this after conquering a new territory. In so doing they populated the new land with people whose loyalty was beyond question. Potentially rebellious peoples were also moved, but to areas with an established loyalty to the empire. Whenever the Incas had occasion to shift populations, they always resettled them at the same elevation and in a climate similar to their previous home.

The plane to Cuzco was a small jet, capable of transporting perhaps a hundred people. I had traveled on such planes before, usually in the United States on regional airlines that catered to businessmen. In Peru, the contrast of the modern jet with its colorful assortment of passengers was startling. The Peruvians piled onto the airplane as if it were a bus. Old men with broken suitcases tied together with rope, children with cardboard boxes and plastic toys, and women with babies tied onto their backs with shawls all clambered up the aluminum stairway and onto the plane. Somehow a young Indian man had convinced the airline officials to allow him to carry on board a crate filled with live chickens. The birds were squawking, their feathers flying from the slats in the wooden crate. Babies were yowling, and people were yelling back and forth to each other. Only the old men were silent. I managed to squeeze into a window seat. When everyone was finally buckled in, the plane rolled onto the runway. Without even a pause we took off.

With my head pressed against the tiny window, I studied the landscape below. For several hours we flew over a series of mountain ridges that, from the air, resembled an old-fashioned washboard. Lines of shadow, like tiger stripes, angled across the gray-green hills. Except for the swift shadow of the plane, nothing moved on the ground below us. For most of the way I didn't see a road. Finally, I picked out a thin, white line, snaking laterally across a mountain ridge, that I presumed to be some sort of pathway through the territory. As my plane flew over the landscape, the accounts of earlier travelers took on new meaning for me.

Less than a hundred years ago, securing a mule train required an application to the governor of Peru. Unless one had considerable influence, such transportation was almost impossible to arrange. Having hired the mule train, one still could not be assured of getting underway. Keeping a close watch over the porters and the mules—keeping the "train" intact up to the moment of departure—was imperative. I could hardly imagine being in a strange country, without benefit of understanding the language, bribing the governor to hire transportation, then having to guard the entire entourage (for which payment was made in advance) to prevent it from vanishing into the countryside. All of this before taking the very first step into the interior, a region fraught with danger of attack from outcast highwaymen and pernicious insects.

In 1901 the author and noted explorer Dr. W. Golden Mortimer described the people of the highlands as

> commonly poor, and viewing all travelers with suspicion. They cannot be counted upon to grant any favors, and even when letters are brought from the provincial government they must be emphasized with "threats." The natural reserve of the Serrano extends to an actual disinclination to grant the slightest hospitality even in their homes, and as a traveler approaches a hut he may often be challenged with the words manam cancha—"we have nothing," even before having expressed a desire for anything, and in some instances before the dwellers have taken the trouble to see who approaches.[1]

From other accounts I had read, a much higher social consciousness had existed in Peru before the Spanish arrival. Father Blas-Valera, the respected New World historian, includes in his list of pre-Columbian laws, "The Law of Hospitality," which prescribed the means of ministering to the necessities of strangers and travelers.[2] According to Von Tschudi, the German explorer of the nineteenth century, "The Inca social institutions were a powerful means to preserve the morality and social virtues of the nation and very justly might Count Carli say in his American letters (Vol. I, pg. 215), that the moral man in Peru was infinitely superior to the European."[3]

In addition to the pre-Columbian municipal laws and the Law of Hospitality was the Law of Brotherhood, a code that set forth the requirement for mutual aid in the cultivation of land and construction of houses. A Law in Favor of Invalids required that the lame, the deaf, the dumb, the blind, the crippled, the decrepit, and the infirm be supported at public expense. This law commanded that two or three times a month these invalids be invited to the festivals or public feasts, so that among the general rejoicing they might forget in some measure their suffering. I conjectured that the coarseness of the Indians' behavior described by later travelers such as Dr. Mortimer could only be the result of mistreatment they had suffered at the hands of their conquerors.

I had read stories and poetry from pre-Columbian times. Though they had been translated into English, these stories still conveyed to me a profound sensitivity, a deep pathos that had survived both the translation and the passing of the centuries. Such was the short poem that the Inca Pachacuti is said to have recited in a low, sad voice just before his end:

> Like a lily in the garden was I born
> And like a lily I grew up.
> As the years passed I grew old,
> And when the time for dying came,
> I withered and I died.[4]

Whenever I encountered a word in Quechua I would pronounce it aloud, harkening to its sound. In the past, when I had thought of traveling to Peru, I viewed it as a pilgrimage to a magical land. So why had I waited so many years to embark on an actual journey to the land whose ancient cultures had so thoroughly captivated my imagination?

Fear had held me back—fear that was connected to my shuddering experience with the black cloud. I had imagined that the flaw in my character made me unworthy of the spiritual truths embodied in the sacred vessel that had summoned my insight. As the years passed, while I worked at UCLA, spoke at Esalen, and made radio appearances, I had gradually gained a sense of self-worth. I felt joyful and fulfilled in my quest. The publication of my theory in journals and in the mainstream press was in some measure a vindication of my initial experience. Most important, sharing the whistles with others had brought intimacy into my life. Finally I was able to gather the courage to undertake the journey to the land that had been calling me.

In less than two hours after take-off, the jet circled a little town nestled in a verdant mountain valley. Agricultural terraces, cut into the sides of the surrounding hills, looked like steps leading down from the sky into the ancient center of Andean life. In Quechua the word *cuzco* means "navel." Historians agree that the name of the city refers to the time when the Inca capital was thought of as "the navel of the world."

Just before landing I caught a glimpse of red tile roofs and church steeples, architectural features added since the Spanish conquest. It didn't matter to me that the city had outwardly changed. Its ancient core remained, and the essential quality I hoped to connect with was intangible.

I checked into the Savoy Hotel, about ten blocks from the main square or plaza. Directly across from the hotel, a small triangular park featured a statue of Pizarro, the Spanish adventurer who had irrevocably changed the face of this city and the destiny of its people. I felt a flash of anger upon seeing the steel image of the man who had wrought such havoc here more than four centuries before.

In the hotel restaurant I ate a lunch comprised of potato and corn soup served with hot rolls. The waiter brought me a steaming pitcher of coca tea, which he said was offered to all new arrivals in Cuzco as a palliative for the high altitude. The tea seemed to work. After lunch I had plenty of energy despite the long flight and extreme change in altitude, so I hired a cab and rode up to Sacsahuaman.

Sacsahuaman. I had read about this megalithic ruin that sits enigmatically just north of the city. Without exception, chroniclers and historians had vied with one another in choosing superlatives to describe the imposing stone wall that is the dominant feature of the monument. Outlandish as it might seem, even the Swiss archaeological sensationalist, Erich Von Daniken, had theorized that the wall had been built by visitors from outer space.

In Quechua, *Sacsahuaman* means "Fill thee falcon." The popular interpretation was that any enemy of the Inca who might presume to attack this fortification would become carrion for falcons. This interpretation seemed strange to me, because it was my understanding that falcons do not eat carrion. I had read that the founder of the Inca dynasty, and all of the Incas down to the Inca Pachacuti, had had a familiar spirit who took the form of a falcon. In addition to it being a military fortification, I believed Sacsahuaman had been a place where the leader of the empire would commune with his guardian spirit.

As we drove toward the monument I got my first down-to-earth view of the old city. The narrow, winding streets were crowded. Every now and then, among the jumble of cars, trucks, and throngs of people, I glimpsed the foundation of a building constructed from finely hewn granite blocks. The old blocks contrasted with the newer—but often meager—structures resting upon them. Despite the change since the conquest, the foundation of the city was still intact.

The road twisted and turned past ramshackle houses and "Inca Cola" signs, past naked children who splashed in mud puddles by the side of the road, past workmen whitewashing a cinderblock wall. Although I was here in Peru, I realized I was still set apart— this time by the glass windshield of the taxi—from the life of the people and the city through which I traveled. But I was getting closer. The taxi stopped. A dilapidated bus had broken down in the middle of a tiny intersection, blocking the narrow street. I could do nothing but wait.

I got out of the car with the driver and ambled over to the scene of the mishap. A wheel had fallen off the bus. No, the tire hadn't gone flat; the lug nuts holding the wheel to the brake drum had somehow worked themselves loose, allowing the wheel to detach. The main cause for the delay was the lack of a jack to lift the bus.

Suddenly I heard a terrific din. Some sort of procession had turned the corner on the next block and was headed our way. It was really more a throng than a procession. Covering both sidewalks and the street itself, several hundred men, women, and children— some with drums and tambourines—accompanied an enormous litter, borne by at least ten men who kept switching places with others from the crowd. On top of the litter was a life-sized figure of a woman wearing a crown. She was dressed in an old-fashioned green velvet dress—of a style from the Victorian era—draped with dozens of gold chains, rhinestone jewelry, and brightly col- ored paper flowers. This was a religious personage, I gathered, and today was her holy day. The broken-down bus thwarted the procession and, in the maneuvering that took place to get the litter past it, the priest in charge halted long enough to swing his burning censer over the wheel lying forlornly in the road. The procession then moved on down the street to the erratic rhythm of drums and tambourines.

At last the jack arrived in an Army Jeep driven by a uniformed soldier complete with steel helmet and carbine. The axle was jacked up high enough to slip the wheel back on, but now the lug nuts were gone. I surmised that the men would remove one or two of the nuts from the other wheels on the bus, but instead they wired the wheel on. Repeatedly they looped what looked like bailing wire through the holes in the wheel rim, wrapping the wire around the naked wheel studs. To my eye the repair was wholly unsatisfactory and downright dangerous. I suspect the soldier who seemed to be in charge of getting the bus rolling again thought so too. Before allowing the bus to proceed, he insisted on looping a nylon rope around the axle and then through the wheel, finishing it all off with a complex knot that he tied with a flourish. The old bus roared back to life and slowly drove away leaving a trail of black smoke. The wheel wobbled slightly from side to side, but the wire and rope held.

We were on our way again as well. After a fifteen-minute drive the cab pulled off the road and onto a grassy plain that divided two hills. I got out of the car and walked toward an enormous wall composed of massive stones. Twenty feet high, the barrier zigzagged for about a third of a mile around the base of one of the hills. I walked up to one of the larger stones set into the wall. The boulder was at least twice the size of an automobile, and each side of it had been sculpted in such a way as to conform precisely to the various rocks adjoining it. The altitude was well above ten thousand feet, and although the coca tea had helped, just walking over to the wall was tiring. The fact that someone had moved these stones (the quarry was on the other side of a river a goodly distance away) and then somehow cut them to fit so precisely together, especially at this altitude, was astounding.

I climbed a staircase beyond a doorway sized for a giant. Nearly out of breath, I reached the top of the hill encircled by the immense wall. Protruding from the earth, foundation stones sketched the outline of three towers that had formerly surmounted the hill. Early chroniclers relate that two square towers were employed as apartments for the garrison, and a circular tower was reserved for the Inca and his family.

Looking out over Cuzco to the south, I remembered a day the previous summer when I had looked over San Francisco Bay from the summit of Mt. Tamalpais, just north of San Francisco. It was the week after my Esalen presentation, when I had driven up the coast to northern California. On the way I had turned off the highway onto a road that wound up the side of the mountain. When I reached the parking area on top, I found a crowd of people holding a festival. It was a diverse group comprised mostly of college students, flower children, and mountain folk, with a smattering of young professionals and their families.

It had been a picture-book day. The view of Berkeley and San Francisco from the towering peak known locally as "Mt. Tam" was breathtaking. At the base of the mountain, San Francisco Bay served as a shimmering blue mirror. Multicolored sails from a flotilla of boats looked like upside-down kites flying on the sea. The air was so clear that the whole scene appeared to be painted, a vibrant watercolor.

From a large wooden bandstand in an outdoor amphitheater at the top of Mt. Tam, the San Francisco Inspirational Choir was belting out a gospel song into the swaying mass of people. Someone was passing through the crowd, pasting little mirrored stars in the middle of everyone's forehead. As the sun beamed down on the dancers, refracted rays of colored light sparkled in every direction. As I joined in, I soon learned this was "The Rainbow Family."

Now in Peru, it was the middle of winter, a rainy time of year in Cuzco. A little pool of water had collected in the exact center of the spot where the circular tower had once stood. I climbed over the carefully arranged rocks that formed the outline of the stone circle, and I knelt by the little pool. Then, to my own amazement, I scooped some water out of the pool with my hands and washed my hair. My act was spontaneous, almost a reflex action. I was not aware of any pre-Columbian hair-washing ceremony, although I had seen a Moche ceramic that depicted a man on a mountain washing his hair. I was glad to be alone, slightly embarrassed by what had just occurred.

Sitting on the edge of the uppermost wall, I let my thoughts drift amidst the ruins of the ancient edifice. Who had built this place, I wondered, to unequivocally assert their mastery of the material realm? Were they the same people who had devised the whistles that led me here? Whoever they were, I felt a deep connection with them.

As I climbed down from my vantage point, I noticed tiny blue and yellow wildflowers growing throughout the ruin. Dragonflies flitted about; I watched one alight just at the juncture where two huge stones were joined. Through the translucent wings of the dragonfly I could see the intricate parting line that separated the ponderous stones. The dragonfly's wings reflected the light, some of which illuminated the huge, hewn stones beneath the insect. Once again I was watching a play of light. As my vision juxtaposed the delicate life form and the mysterious wall, the miracle of each—and of everything—was revealed.

Wherever you are,
There!
Is the entry point.

—Kabir

THE NEXT MORNING AFTER BREAKFAST I walked to the Cuzco market. As I made my way through the crowded streets, I was inundated by a variety of smells and splashes of vivid color. It seemed as if everything imaginable were for sale, from pots and pans to ancient locks. Rows of Indian women sat behind mounds of produce, and hordes of children hawked packages of Chiclets for two cents apiece. Venders implored everyone who passed to buy, holding up weavings with designs I recognized from my study of pre-Columbian art. I saw a man with an old-fashioned typewriter who had set up his business on a window ledge (to type your letter for a fee), and I noticed a wooden table made in the seventeenth century that would have commanded a small fortune in a New York art gallery. This was exactly the sort of antique Barbara and I had been in search of when I'd driven to that auction barn back in Pennsylvania. In Cuzco, however, the table served only to display an old leather harness and a burlap bag half-full of cement.

The sights and smells reminded me of an outdoor farmers mar-

ket I had frequented with my mother and my paternal grandmother when I was a child. I would wend my way through throngs
of people, a veritable forest of overcoats and shopping bags, holding onto my grandmother's hand, fearful of being separated from
her in the crowd. Invariably we stopped at the fish market. I liked
the smell of the sawdust on the floor of the store, and I was fascinated by the rows of dead fish on ice, with their glassy eyes and
blood-red gills. In Wilmington, the produce had been stacked
along the curb, sold out of the back of old panel trucks or displayed on rickety card tables or wooden crates. The men and
women selling vegetables were weather beaten, I imagined, from
the hard lives they lived working on their farms. Once, my younger
sister Diane and I bought some fresh corn at the outdoor market
and learned to our chagrin that it was necessary to peel back the
husk to check for worms. When we got home with our purchase,
we discovered that half the kernels on each ear had already been
eaten.

I saw husked corn in the Cuzco market with kernels nearly the
size of a nickel. Women sold it boiled and ready to eat along with
a kind of soft, white cheese, or *queso,* as they called it. A woman
tending a five-gallon can perched over a few charcoals sold me a
piece of grilled fish along with some rice, all of which she drenched
in a fragrant yellow sauce. The woman served the fish to me on a
paper plate that she made on the spot, neatly tearing the paper
from a brown shopping bag. I sat on a wooden crate nearby and ate
an early lunch; it was delicious. For dessert, I bought a couple of
donuts that had been fried in a can of oil—also heated over charcoals—and then rolled in granulated white sugar.

From a wizened old man selling potions and charms, I bought
two measures of copal. Carefully, so as not to spill any of the resinous
crystals of gum, he twisted the aromatic incense into a piece of
newspaper as I stared with morbid fascination at the dried fetus of

a llama in the midst of his wares. The llama fetus had been employed as a charm from pre-Columbian times, buried under the cornerstone of a new building for luck. I wondered how it related to a real medicine like quinine that had been discovered in Peru and sold here for centuries by generations of folk healers.

In a whitewashed building at the end of a dirt lane, I found the government store where coca leaves were sold. The store's interior was dark, lit only by the light that filtered through several small windows and the open doorway. A large woman wearing a voluminous apron presided over wicker baskets and wooden bins that contained the faintly aromatic leaves. I bought several ounces for less than a dollar. The woman scooped the coca out of a basket before weighing and then securing the leaves in a plastic bag. As I left the store, an old man approached me. His deeply creased face resembled the cracked surface of a dry lakebed. Extending his hand, he silently asked for a gift. I reached into my bag and gave the man a handful of coca leaves.

Speaking rapidly in Spanish, the woman minding the store called me back into the building, where she handed me a black lump of something that looked like a little piece of coal. *"Tokra,"* she said, repeating the unknown word several times while pointing at the black nugget. Detecting my confusion, the woman retrieved the lump and bit off a tiny corner of it with her teeth. Taking the little piece out of her mouth, she pantomimed placing it into a few leaves, and then made the motion of putting the entire concoction into her mouth. It was then I realized that this was the alkali or lime-like substance needed to efficiently extract the alkaloids from the coca leaf. I thanked the woman for the tokra and walked through the market chewing several dozen leaves, adding tokra as she had instructed. Within ten minutes I could feel a growing numbness in my mouth and an increase in energy.

For centuries, Indians in highland communities have chewed

coca leaves to increase their endurance and to ease the burdens of their lives. Greatly revered for its magical and nutritive value, coca is still referred to as the "divine plant of the Incas." As I chewed the leaves, I felt a growing sense of well-being; it was that rare feeling of moving in harmony with the world around me. The clouds in the sky, the light breeze in the air, and the people whom I passed on the street all seemed to be moving in tune with the natural order. I felt myself to be a part of the whole.

The feeling I was experiencing was not unknown to me. Satiated in the embrace of a lover, I had felt a similar feeling of total well-being. What I was feeling now, however, was not the same dream-like bliss, but rather a kind of super-consciousness, where I was acutely aware of a myriad of subtle perceptions.

In the 1960s I had spent a crystalline day in a tiny park outside of Wilmington, my perceptions altered by 250 micrograms of a new chemical produced by a Swiss pharmaceutical company. On that day, too, I had experienced the perfection of my life. As I walked through the park I perceived the subtle rhythm of nature. Everything was in tune: the flowers and the clouds, the grass swaying in the breeze, and the people relaxing on the lawn. It was a Sunday, and at one point during the day I could clearly see the futility of my unrelenting battle in the world of commerce. Business was a contrivance, I realized; it was out of sync with the natural order of life. Perhaps I wouldn't go back to fighting the traffic and the struggle for contracts to keep the machine shop busy. Nevertheless, I had returned to work the following Tuesday, my idealistic vision fading in the light of my compulsions.

Now, as I walked the streets of Cuzco, I thought about another garden: the legendary garden in the Incas' holiest shrine, the Temple of the Sun. That garden had been wrought entirely of silver and gold. Temple artisans had reproduced every type of plant and animal so exquisitely that one traveler had described it "as if a dream had come to life." The Spanish soldiers had harvested a field of golden corn with silver leaves and tassels made of golden threads, casting it all into the crucible with the rest of their plunder. As I walked toward the Temple of the Sun, I looked into the faces of the people I passed on the street—Indians whose ancestors had lost their civilization in the conquest. Some of them resembled the portraits I had studied on the old clay pots.

Here and there an aquiline nose or lofty brow reminded me that these people were descendants of the Incas. The men, of medium stature with jet-black hair, wore ponchos and loose-fitting trousers turned up nearly to the knees. I surmised that they turned up their pant legs to avoid the splashing of mud from the large puddles that were everywhere along the street. Many of the men carried bundles on their backs, supported by a strap looped around the forehead. More often than not, a rough sandal revealed a gnarled foot, like the twisted root of an old tree. The women wore full skirts tied at the waist with brightly colored sashes. Broad-brimmed hats made of felt or straw kept the equatorial sun from their faces as they bargained in the market.

A military government ruled Peru, and the police wore Army uniforms. Each man carried a carbine. I knew nothing about the country's political situation, but everyone seemed to smile easily, and I sensed no fear or anger. Some of the barefoot children, though, seemed like tragic characters from a Dickens' novel rather than people living in the twentieth century. Their clothing made from patched and tattered rags, little boys and girls begged incessantly from doorways and on street corners. None seemed hungry, but their poverty and lack of hope reflected a misery I had not expected.

About a block from the Temple of the Sun, I crossed a street and wondered if this had been the boundary where, in Inca times, everyone was required to remove their shoes before proceeding any further toward the sacred shrine. I was approaching the spiritual heart of the old empire. Whether it was historians' descriptions or the effect of the coca leaves, I felt a growing excitement upon reaching the Incas' principal house of worship. The exterior wall of the temple was made of granite blocks that fit so tightly together it appeared as if a single stone had been etched to create a huge mosaic. After paying a few hundred soles, the equivalent of a little more than a dollar, I entered the sanctuary and gazed at the blank, stone walls that surrounded a nearly deserted courtyard.

Two young boys who were playing next to a dry fountain in the center of the courtyard offered to give me a tour. I accepted. Water for the fountain had once run through gold and silver pipes. The Spanish had ripped out these precious pipes and melted them down for shipment to Spain. Once again I felt a flash of anger toward the invaders who had plundered this country, forcing its children to play around a dry fountain in the center of their spiritual inheritance. The boys took me through a series of rooms made from the same polished granite as the rest of the temple. Stripped of their former magnificence, the rooms now seemed like stone cells. The now-barren cubicles formerly had served as sanctuaries, tended with devotion, and dedicated to the heavenly bodies and to the rainbow.

In addition to the priests chosen from the royal family, a special class of astronomers also had lived in the temple. These men studied the zodiac, calculated the equinox and solstice, predicted eclipses and marked the passing of the seasons. The temple was envisioned as the center of a conceptual wheel, called the *ceque,* with spokes radiating toward the horizon. Hundreds of holy sites were located on the ground along these imaginary lines. Each line corresponded to the rising and setting of certain stars. Each site was honored on a special day of the year and was cared for by a different Cuzco family. Thus, the movement of the celestial bodies became a part of the community's life, a conscious integration of everyone's daily existence with the cosmic reality.

I found a terrace on the east side of the temple. The terrace overlooked the area where the precious garden had once stood. I walked around a sort of outdoor gallery to the back of the present day Church of Santo Domingo. At the end of the terrace I came upon a pile of rubble. Two Indian workmen, covered with dirt, looked up at me from the bottom of a trench they were digging along the outer wall of the church. Spontaneously I offered them some coca from the bag in my pocket. Both men scrambled out of the hole, and one of the men, taking the coca in his hands, raised it toward the sun overhead. He murmured a few words in Quechua and blew his breath over the leaves in his hands. For a moment I felt as if I had been transported into the past.

For hundreds of years coca had been an essential part of a daily devotional ceremony in the sanctuary, but I don't think the man's gesture was a conscious re-enactment of the ancient ritual. Although its origin may have been based on the Inca practice, the man's prayer was simply his customary way of giving thanks for the blessing of the leaf. The fact that we were standing in the Inca's most sacred shrine was incidental. Unable to speak their language, I could not communicate verbally with the men, but sharing the leaves with them was a communion that went beyond words. The man's prayer provided a basis for my sense of brotherhood with both men, and was for me another echo from a distant time when the temple pulsated as the heart of the empire.

Leaving the terrace, I returned to the room that had served as the special sanctuary dedicated to the sun. I sat on the floor with my back against the smoothly hewn granite blocks of the west wall. At one time an enormous gold disk had reflected the sun's rays into the room. The room had been filled with radiant light, enhanced and magnified by golden panels affixed to the walls and to the ceiling. Now I leaned against cold granite in the dull, gray shadows.

In the Temple of the Sun, I closed my eyes and visualized the pageantry of Inti-Raymi, the solstice ceremony. Celebrated as the most important religious service of the year, the ceremony was actually begun three days before the solstice day with a fast by the entire population. Every fire in the realm was extinguished. In this manner, everyone's attention was sharply focused on the impending moment. On the morning of the sacred day, the Inca and his family congregated with the priests in the temple courtyard. Using a polished obsidian mirror, the chief priest focused the first rays of the rising sun onto a specially woven piece of cloth that had been sanctified for the ceremony. The magnified rays ignited the cloth and, with it, a new fire for the nation.

Although I sat for hours on the earthen floor of the shrine, nothing dramatic occurred. No vision of secret rites or spirits of Inca priests appeared to me. Gradually, though, the underlying meaning of the sun ceremony and the other rituals that had been celebrated there became clear to me. The old Indian practices were, I concluded, the active participation—by a highly evolved people—in the very clockwork of the universe. The Incas had discerned that, through their conscious participation in the natural order, they could in some measure support the orderly sequence of life. Their ceremonial recognition of cyclical events was an act of attention designed to support the balance and harmony of the whole.

The concept was simple yet profound. The single Hebrew prayer I could remember from my youth was the "Shema," which proclaims the unity of God with the whole of Creation. "Hear, oh Israel: the Lord our God, the Lord is One." The Andean cosmology embraced the same concept: The universe is interwoven, and man is not excluded but inextricably connected to the whole. God could not be a separate entity apart from his Creation; God was dynamically infused throughout the whole of existence. I imagined this was what Jesus had meant when he said, "I and my Father are One."

As I left the Inca temple I noticed a small downy feather on the ground. I picked it up and blew the feather into the air from the palm of my hand. It was my way to honor what had once transpired within the old sanctuary. At that precise moment another Indian came around the corner. The man was obviously on an errand, carrying in his hands a single, highly polished, black Army boot. In a glance, he saw me blow the feather into the air. Changing direction, the Indian approached me. Speaking rapidly, he said something in Spanish that I did not understand, so I asked a passing tourist if she would translate for me.

"This man is telling you the ancient spirits are still here," she informed me with a look of surprise. "He says that even though the Spaniards have stolen the golden sun from their temple, the old spirits are still here ... in the air ... and in the water...."

Before I could gather my thoughts or thank him, the man turned and walked away. For a moment I wondered if I had imagined the entire interaction, but I couldn't have fabricated something as odd as a man holding a lone Army boot. In some manner the episode felt comforting, as though the spirits the man described were welcoming me to the heart of the Inca Empire.

At the end of the week I bought a railroad ticket to Machu Picchu. As I traveled on the antiquated train through the Peruvian countryside I reviewed my odyssey. So far my feeling was one of immense relief. Although nothing momentous had occurred during my trip, nothing terrible had happened either. I was comfortable, really at ease, in this land and with these people whose ancestors had made the whistling vessels. It would be wonderful, I thought, to bring the instruments back to Peru and play them here. But that possibility seemed remote. Pre-Columbian art was now considered a national treasure, and it was illegal to take artifacts out of the country. If I returned to Peru with my collection of whistles, in all likelihood they would be confiscated before I ever had a chance to play them in the ruins.

Almost immediately the train ride absorbed my attention. After negotiating a number of switchbacks to scale a precipitous grade, we followed the Huarocondo River until it reached the Urubamba Valley, with its turbulent river of the same name. Small villages and farms dotted the countryside. The train stopped several times, allowing enterprising villagers to walk the length of each car. Indian women with their children crowded on board selling steaming ears of the same boiled corn and soft, white cheese I had seen in the Cuzco market. They also sold fresh-picked cherries. At first this activity seemed so chaotic it appeared that one or another of the children would be left on the train as it pulled away from a stop. This was not the case, however. Evidently what I viewed as disorder was a daily rhythm in the life of these people.

For a moment my thoughts flashed back to Barbara and her children. They were half a world apart from the women and children here. I pictured Barbara chauffeuring Chip and Devon to school in Unionville and then after school driving them to a riding lesson or to hockey practice. Despite the chaos of my inner life then, a part of me longed for the warmth we had shared as a family. I missed the children. I wondered whether I was remembered as the man with the gold Cadillac and my schemes to control African mines. I wondered whether Barbara and the children would ever understand why I had to leave. As the train passed through the Peruvian countryside, I felt a deep thankfulness for the chance I had been given to start over again.

Leaving the agricultural part of the valley, we entered a canyon cut by the tumultuous river. A seething, churning cascade, at times only a few feet from the roadbed, the Urubamba seemed as if it could wash the train from its tracks at any moment. The vegetation also changed. Tropical plants and thick vines hung from the cliffs that formed the increasingly narrow gorge. Now and then a brilliant bloom of color dotted the verdant green wall that rose into mountainous heights. This was the fringe of the Amazon that was known as "the eyebrow of the jungle" and the modern approach to Machu Picchu. Supposedly a secret Inca road traced the line of mountains high above us and stretched for more than a thousand miles north to Ecuador. Machu Picchu had remained hidden for nearly four centuries, and no one knew who had inhabited it—or for what purpose—before or after the Spanish conquest.

The train stopped briefly at Kilometer-88 to discharge several people with backpacks who planned to hike the last section of the famous Inca Trail. I hoped to return to Peru and hike the trail myself, but for the present I was content to watch the scenery from the open window of the moving train. About a mile before reaching our destination, the train stopped. A landslide had blocked the track with boulders; until they were removed, we could go no further. Everyone disembarked and, skirting the rocks, began to walk along the tracks. It was a warm, humid morning. Steam from the rains that had caused the rockslide rose into the air from the lush tropical vegetation.

Upon reaching the station, I learned that all but two of the minibus fleet that provided transportation to the top of the mountain had been stranded by another landslide. The bus that was still in service could take me about half the distance, but to reach the legendary city at the summit, I would have to walk the rest of the way.

As I walked up the steep road beyond the drop-off point, I thought it curious that the Incas had not used the wheel in any of their endeavors. Although the fabled Inca roads were exten-

sive and smooth, the Indians employed no cart or wheeled conveyance of any kind. The discovery of a small number of wheeled
children's toys in association with burials confirmed the fact that
the pre-Columbian Andean people could conceptualize and fashion wheels. As far as anyone knew, however, wheels had not been
employed in the making of pottery, in farming, or in construction. In light of this fact, the Incas' megalithic architectural achieve-
ments were an even deeper mystery. The question of how these
people had transported great blocks of granite from their quar-
ries to their building sites remains unanswered.

Somewhere I had learned an intriguing theory that the Andean
civilization had been denied the use of the wheel not by failure
of invention but by religious prohibition. Whoever had set forth the
tenets of life in the region had wanted the people to develop a
more profound approach to working in the material realm than
would be encouraged by the mechanization that would naturally
evolve from the use of the wheel .

Nearly out of breath from the climb, I reached the famous Inca
ruin before anyone else from the train. Spellbound, I sat and stared
in wonder at the sight before me. The hidden city was a master-
piece, a granite-hewn jewel that transcended the pale shadows
captured in a thousand photographs. Each wall, terrace, and stairway blended into a harmonious whole, a silent symphony that
enveloped me in its perfection. Trance-like, I walked through the
deserted buildings and climbed a staircase hewn from a single
boulder. The antithesis of the Mayan ruins with their carved inscrip-
tions, Machu Picchu contained not one syllable or glyph to hint
at its intended purpose. Nakedly itself, the mountaintop city was
its own explanation. The scholarly questions dissolved into the
vision, obliterated by the ardent reality. Only a devotion sublime
could have prompted an undertaking such as this, and only a realization of profound love could have sustained and completed it.

Over the course of the next four days I explored. Beginning early in the morning, before the arrival of the tourists, I wandered amidst the terraces, galleries, and ingenious masonry constructions. Time and again I found myself drawn to the somber cave beneath the city's central tower. The entrance to the cave, an angled slab of white granite sculpted with obvious purpose, beckoned with mystery. Although the event had been forgotten, I felt certain that whatever it was that had initiated Machu Picchu's inspired construction had occurred on or beneath that immense rock. This was the heart of the old sanctuary. I entered the cave and sat in a life-sized niche. This place was like Stonehenge, Teotihuacán, or the Great Pyramid in Egypt, I imagined, where an unknown energy of mysterious purpose had called out to inspire a human being to an act of great majesty.

To avoid the chatter of the tourists during the crowded midday hours, I explored the various paths leading out of the city. One morning, as I followed the Inca Trail from the main gate, I was startled by the piercing screech of two parrots that flew from a small tree alongside the path. In Quechua these birds are called *huacamayas*, a term that translates as "guardians of the sacred." I wondered if the two pale green birds were descended from a pair left by the original occupants of Machu Picchu to guard the path into their sanctuary.

I arose early on the last morning of my stay. Skipping breakfast, I walked alone into the timeless ruin. The sun had not yet risen over the eastern range of mountains as I climbed the evenly spaced terraces that overlook the vast gulf of the Urubamba Valley gorge. Mist clung to the hillside, deepening the aura of mystery that pervaded the silent city. The sanctity and wholeness I had experienced here were now a part of me. Wherever my path might lead, I hoped I might carry with me a trace from the atmosphere of that granite sanctuary. As I gazed out over the gorge, my thoughts returned to

California and the uncertainty of my life there. My academic work was completed, and I knew I had reached another turning point.

It was a chilly morning on the mountain. Reaching into the pocket of my jacket I found a tissue folded around a downy feather given to me by a friend in Los Angeles to leave in some special place in Peru. In my shirt pocket was another feather I had retrieved from a rocky crevice on one of my walks out of the city. Taking both feathers in one hand, I made a wish of unformed words, a silent hope to find a purpose and direction for my life. Repeating the gesture I had made at the Temple of the Sun in Cuzco, I blew the two bits of fluff from my palm and watched as they drifted on a breeze down into the valley below.

Suddenly the stillness was broken by a loud *whoosh*. An immense bird, the largest I had ever seen, swooped directly over my head from behind. An Andean Condor streaked down into the gorge, as if to catch my little feathers and my unformed dream. I held my breath, or perhaps it stopped of its own accord, as I stared at the wondrous creature before me.

Within a few seconds the condor began to soar, and my vision bridged the distance between us. No longer was I separate, the watcher on the mountain, but rather I was an intimate passenger riding upon the bird's back. I could feel the tremor of its huge wings as they stroked the morning mist to lift us up and out of the valley. Finally, in a single instant, the condor disappeared from my vision as it flew directly into the rising sun. Awestruck in the quintessential perfection of the moment, daring not to move or take a breath, I began to weep. And my tears fell to the dark brown earth.

Does the eagle know what is in the pit, or wilt thou ask the mole? Can wisdom be found in a silver rod, or love in a golden bowl?

— *Thel's Motto*

Tucked away on a side street in west Los Angeles, the Santa Monica Mold Shop appeared to be just another one of the thousands of small shops that comprise the industrial complex of southern California. George Binkele's workshop, however, was unlike any other shop I had ever entered. A layer of stark white dust covered everything from floor to ceiling, making the room seem celestial and lending a serene, otherworldly dimension to the hundreds of figurines that crowded the tables and shelves. Pottery birds and mice peeked out at me from behind a woman's skirt embossed on an old-fashioned cookie jar. A raccoon stared vacantly at a duck that had permanently nested on the cover of a soup tureen.

"This will be an ice carving," Mr. Binkele informed me as I approached his workbench.

I admired the two-foot-high clay figure the stocky man was working on. It was a cornucopia overflowing with ripe fruit. Then I looked up at the craftsman to whom I had previously spoken on the telephone. "How does that get from clay to ice?" I asked.

"Plastic," the man replied, carefully tucking a wooden tool he'd been using into the breast pocket of his white lab coat. Binkele turned toward me and took a moment to clean his eyeglasses with a tissue. Then he answered my question. "I'm making this model for a company that will use it to produce plastic molds to sell to restaurants and hotels. The molds are filled with water and then left in one of those walk-in freezers. After the whole thing's frozen, the plastic is cut away to reveal the ice sculpture. It's like an oversized Popsicle," he concluded with a grin.

"I always thought those things were carved by the chef," I replied, remembering the enormous ice sculpture on the buffet table at the Hotel DuPont back in Wilmington. "It was a mystery to me how so many chefs could be sculptors as well."

"Well, at least that mystery's solved," Mr. Binkele answered with a smile. I handed him the Peruvian artifact we had discussed on the phone. For several minutes the moldmaker examined the old pot, turning it carefully in his hands.

"You can still see the potter's thumbprint under this strap handle," he remarked. "It's where he had to compress the clay when he was assembling the vessel." Then Binkele blew into the pot to hear the whistle.

"The challenge would be to get the right sound," he mused, half to himself. "During the firing the clay would shrink and the pitch of the whistle would change. That difference would have to be taken into account."

Then the craftsman seemed to back away from the challenge. "I'm not taking on any new accounts," the man stated, handing me back my artifact. "I have more than enough work from my old customers to keep me busy. I don't know when I could ever get around to a project like this. Anyway, I wouldn't know how to begin to get the sound you want."

I was disappointed. I had already spoken to nearly everyone in the pottery business in Los Angeles. It seemed that my only hope of reproducing the whistles was George Binkele.

I'd had a revelation on my return flight from Peru. I would make whistles. I was so excited by the idea I could barely sleep on the long plane ride home. Pottery was still an active craft. I would search until I found someone who could teach me the skills I would need to recapture the sacred technology. Even if I devoted my entire life to proving my point to the academic community, my work would amount to only a few more pages in the university's research library. On the other hand, if replica instruments were available for people to play, perhaps the original purpose of the old whistles would be rediscovered.

I didn't know how many vessels constituted a "set," but from my experience, seven was an ideal number to play in meditations. During my study of the ancient cultures, I had learned that the number considered most sacred and invoked in rituals in both pre-Columbian as well as modern times was the number seven. Also, I had noticed seven niches in the stone wall behind the main altar at Machu Picchu. Although no one knew what the niches had originally held, they were about the right size for each of them to have contained a whistle pot. I decided to make sets of seven instruments. Before I could make a set of tuned instruments, though, I needed Mr. Binkele's help to make the very first vessel.

"If we could reproduce the sound, what would be involved in making the molds?" I asked, thinking that, if I engaged Mr. Binkele more deeply in the discussion, another avenue of possibility might become evident. I was also curious to learn something about the process.

"The first thing would be to carve a clay model of the piece, oversized to allow for shrinkage in the clay," he answered. "Then we'd cast a master mold from the model, make 'blocks and cases' from the master mold, and finally make the production molds from the blocks. You would need at least three separate molds to make each pot and a fourth mold for the whistle cavity. Look here," he said, retrieving the vessel from me. "You'd need a mold to make the figure, another mold for this back section that looks like a bottle and a third mold for this handle or bridge. You'd have to put the sections together along with the little round cavity that makes the whistle. But I don't know how you'd get the different sounds you want."

Then Mr. Binkele answered his own question. "You would have to make a different mold for each of the sounds. You could vary the size of the whistle cavity as you assembled each pot. That would give you the different notes. The little cavity would have to be positioned exactly or it wouldn't whistle," the craftsman added, returning the old instrument to me.

The moldmaker's detailed explanation cast the specter of an endless series of steps, each taking weeks or perhaps months to complete. A vertiginous feeling of helplessness arose within me. I felt my dream slipping away. Unless I could interest this man in my project, I might never be able to construct even one whistle, let alone reproduce tuned sets of instruments. Suddenly I felt inspired to ask Mr. Binkele if I could work along with him. Perhaps I could help him in some small way so he would have time for my project. As I began my plea, Jim Croce's song, "Time in a Bottle," began to play on the radio that was perched on a shelf over the workbench.

"Mr. Binkele," I said respectfully, looking at the cornucopia the man had been working on, "your carving for the ice sculpture is beautiful. It's a work of art. People will admire and enjoy it." I hesitantly added, "But you're making a mold for a sculpture that will melt."

I paused, desperately hoping I hadn't angered the kindly man who had invited me into his workshop. "This vessel is a thousand years old," I continued, looking down at the black earthenware figurine in my hands. "More than anything else in the world, I want to reproduce it. I'm convinced it's a valuable tool left to us by an advanced civilization. My experience with this vessel has completely changed my life. Honestly, I feel that working with you is my next step.

"Please help me to realize my dream, Sir. I'll work with you under any condition … every day…. I don't care how long it takes or how much it costs," I exclaimed. "I have to do it!"

I was somewhat embarrassed by my presumptuous speech. I half-expected Mr. Binkele to throw me out of his shop. Instead, the stocky man retrieved the Chimú whistle pot and once again turned it over in his capable hands.

"Eventually everything melts," the moldmaker said quietly. Then he retreated to some faraway place behind his eyes. Perhaps he was thinking of the potter or the moldmaker who, so many centuries before, had made the mold for the earthenware vessel that he was now holding. Or maybe George was remembering his early years in Illinois when he, too, had started out with a vision before coming to California to build a business and raise a family.

Finally, Mr. Binkele returned from his reverie and took a moment to study the calendar on the wall over his workbench. Turning from the calendar, he narrowed his gaze as he looked at me. "I have some open time toward the end of May," he said determinedly. "If you come in on the 23rd, Monday morning, we'll have a go at it."

The hollow clay ball lay in my hand like a dark chocolate marble. In less than a minute its color faded to a light tan as the water in the damp clay evaporated. Holding the fragile sphere gently, I carefully drilled a hole, about three-sixteenths of an inch in diameter, through the thin wall of the little clay casting. Too much pressure, I had learned to my dismay, would crumble the delicate sphere, sending a shower of clay shavings onto the floor of the workshop. I carefully positioned the hollow ball onto a pottery vase that George had modified so I could hold the little whistle chamber and still blow into it. Then I gently rotated the casting until the focused air stream from my breath flooded the cavity. As the piercing sound of the whistle filled the shop, all my uncertainty dissolved in an instant. The road ahead might be strewn with obstacles, but I no longer doubted I would eventually reach my goal.

It was Binkele's idea to use a marble as the model for our mold. "I used to have some of those big glass ones around here," he remarked, after rummaging around the shop for a few minutes. "I don't know where they are now. Maybe one of the kids got 'em.

"If you buy a marble tomorrow morning we'll make a mold from it. We can try an idea I've been thinking about for casting the little cavity you need for the whistle. Pick up one of those plastic squeeze bottles, too," he added. "The kind they put ketchup in."

"How about if we use a ball bearing instead of a marble as the model for our mold?" I asked. "If your idea works we can buy bearings of several sizes and then vary them precisely to get the exact tones I'd like to reproduce. I still have access to the UCLA lab. I'll bet we can duplicate the tones exactly."

"There's an idea," Binkele agreed. "A ball bearing would work just as well as a marble."

The moldmaker sat down on a wooden stool by the workbench and began to fiddle with the radio, looking for the station that would broadcast the Dodger game later that afternoon. Then he explained a bit more of the process. "The main problem in casting a hollow figure that's so small is in the removal of the liquid clay—

it's called 'slip'—from inside the mold cavity. When you pour the slip into the mold, the plaster mold absorbs the water from the clay slurry, leaving a thin layer of hardened clay stuck to the inside of the mold. As time goes on, more and more water is absorbed by the plaster mold," he explained. "The longer you leave the slip in the mold, the thicker that clay wall becomes. The idea is to get the wall to the thickness you need, then empty the remaining slip from the mold. That's what makes the piece hollow," he concluded.

"What would happen if you didn't empty the mold?" I asked.

"If you didn't empty the mold all the water in the slip would eventually be absorbed by the plaster," Binkele replied. "You'd end up with a solid clay figure. The piece would be very heavy, use up a lot more clay and take a lot longer to dry. A solid figurine would also have a tendency to crack. You wouldn't get much of a sound out of a solid clay figure," he added, with a twinkle in his eyes, "and it's a pretty slow way to make marbles."

"I don't know if there's any demand for clay marbles these days," I bantered back. "So what's the problem in making the little whistle cavity?" I asked, becoming serious again. "Can't we just pour the excess slip out of the mold in the same way we pour it in?"

"Normally you can pour it out the same way, through the fill hole," the moldmaker replied. "With larger castings the clay build-up on the inside of the mold doesn't interfere with emptying it. That's how we'll do it when we cast the larger pieces of your vessel. When you cast something as small as a marble, however, the fill hole has to be tiny. As the clay sets up in the mold, the hardened clay is likely to close the little fill hole as well. Then there wouldn't be a way to empty it.

"The plastic ketchup bottle might be our solution," he explained. "We'll squeeze the clay into the mold with the bottle and then reverse the process when we're ready to empty the mold.

Releasing the pressure from the sides of the plastic bottle should produce sufficient suction to draw the remaining slip out of the mold, even through a tiny fill hole," he added. "You'll need to do some finishing on the little hollow ball so it will whistle, but that shouldn't be too difficult for someone with your determination."

I wasn't sure if George was teasing me, but I was certain that without the benefit of this kindly man's patience and expertise, I could not have accomplished this seemingly simple task. Over a period of weeks we must have cast hundreds of little hollow balls. For me, it was an important lesson in timing. If I began to work on the whistle too soon after it came out of the mold, the soft clay would tear or distort from the pressure of my tools. If I waited too long, the fragile cavity would become brittle and crack while I was working on it. By storing the little castings in a plastic box with some moist paper, I could regulate the respiration of the clay and work in a more relaxed manner.

The orientation of the clay cavity to the air stream was the most critical variable. Even the slightest change in position affected the quality of the sound. It was a near-maddening process, punctuated by moments of utter frustration, but finally I learned. I varied the size of the opening in each casting. After firing the castings, I measured their sounds with the spectrum analyzer at UCLA. Eventually I determined the exact dimensions of the cavities and their openings I needed to produce the tones I wanted to recreate. Weeks passed as George led me through the process of making the molds. During this time we grew closer, and I knew the mold-maker also shared in my sense of accomplishment.

Now and then I would walk out of the shop and play a note on one of my whistles. As the clear, piercing sound rang out into the air, I experienced a feeling of such great happiness that sometimes tears would fill my eyes. In a modern world seemingly driven by technology, in a city where the aerospace industry was producing vehicles to carry men into space, I had found fulfillment in the making of a simple clay whistle.

On the day before the summer solstice, I interrupted my work with George and headed for the Rainbow Family's annual healing gathering. Even though a year had passed since my first encounter with the family on Mt. Tam, I was still convinced that it was important for me to share the old whistles with this New Age group of people. I had learned that this year the family's annual convocation would be held in a remote wilderness area of southern New Mexico. I was intrigued that the group called their festival a healing gathering. Many members of the family were practitioners of various healing arts such as herbal medicine or massage therapy. Still, I wasn't really sure what actually went on at a healing gathering; I imagined I would find out.

As I crossed the California desert and drove into Arizona I was excited to be on another adventure. It was the day of the solstice, and I fantasized about the reception that both the ancient whistles and I would be given at the Rainbow Gathering. From what I had observed on Mt. Tam, the Rainbow Family was comprised of people who would be most receptive to experiencing alternative realities or spiritually induced states of consciousness. Perhaps I would find a place within this family as well. Absorbed in thought, the miles passed quickly. Late in the afternoon, I pulled my truck into the Eden Hot Springs in Stafford, Arizona, where I planned to spend the night before proceeding to the gathering the next day.

Formerly known as "Healing Waters" to the Native Americans of the Southwest, Eden Hot Springs had undergone great change since the arrival of the settlers. During the late nineteenth century an investment group had developed the hot mineral springs into a spa and hotel. Now, however, the run-down buildings were being used as the home for a commune. A number of other people had stopped at the springs on their way to the Rainbow Family gathering; within a short time after my arrival I met another traveler.

Michael-John was a lean man in his mid-thirties who told me he had spent a lot of time on the road as an itinerant sign painter. When I met Michael-John he was wearing faded Levis, a brightly colored Guatemalan shirt, and a gray felt hat with a feather jauntily stuck in his hatband. The man had a clear look in his eyes, as if he had done a lot of fasting or adhered to a Spartan vegetarian diet. I was only mildly surprised when he told me he not only was a member of the Rainbow Family but served as a spiritual focalizer for them as well. In the course of our conversation, I told him about the whistles from Peru that I was bringing to the gathering. On this day of the solstice, we agreed that we should play the old instruments to commemorate the occasion.

Together we assembled a small group on the lawn of the dilapidated, turn-of-the-century hotel. Forming a circle, seven of us began to play. Like the wind-borne hum of thousands of cicadas in a summer field, the combined tones filled the air with their pervasive effect. After a few moments it was impossible to determine the real source of the low, pulsating sensation that wavered like an electric current inside my head.

Huge cottonwoods surrounded the decaying building, which glowed golden yellow in the late afternoon sunlight. Looking around, I felt an air of timelessness to this place, valued by Native American and settler alike for its healing waters. After a few minutes, a glistening black snake, at least four feet long, crawled out of the underbrush. Making its way across the lawn, the creature passed very close to our circle and, to everyone's astonishment, climbed the cottonwood tree under which we were sitting. When it reached the first large branch that extended over our group, the reptile slithered out on the branch, stopped, raised its head, and looked down at us.

Amazed, all of us stopped playing our instruments. The snake didn't move. Had we charmed it? I remembered from my reading that in South America the snake is often viewed as an agent or harbinger of transformation. Shedding its outer skin, the inner snake is reborn. Since they have this ability to seemingly transform themselves, serpents are considered powerful allies in the supernatural pantheon of the *curandero* or native folk healer.

This dramatic symbol of change appearing at our solstice meditation felt auspicious. I viewed the reptile's startling behavior as a sign. Perhaps it was confirmation of a new chapter in my quest initiated by the flight of the condor and forwarded by my meeting and working with Mr. Binkele. Working with Mr. Binkele, though, seemed to have more to do with outer manifestation. I wondered, Did this nearly surreal experience foretell the coming of yet another change within myself?

Early the next morning, I left the commune and reached Silver City, New Mexico, just before noon. A few miles outside of town, I turned onto a dirt forest road and followed it for about twenty miles into the mountains. Along the way, an occasional cardboard sign painted with rainbows confirmed I was heading in the right direction. A few miles after crossing the continental divide, the road ended at a cleared parking area in the heart of the Gila National Park. Leaving my truck, I set out on foot into the rugged wilderness.

It was a clear, sunny day, and on one side of the path, sandstone cliffs towered into the absolute blueness of the New Mexico sky. A small stream meandered along the floor of the canyon. Eventually tall pines took the place of the sandstone escarpment. The trees shaded the trail from the hot southwest sun until the canyon gradually widened into a meadow. As I walked into the gathering, people from every side greeted me warmly, "Welcome home, brother."

I explored a side canyon with its own stream where I found a good spot for a campsite. After pitching my tent, I walked around the area to see what was going on. The scene was reminiscent of the 1960s. Here was the vanguard of the American counterculture camped in a pristine mountainous wilderness. These were the people who had demonstrated against the war in Vietnam. They had emerged from the disillusionment of American politics with the conviction to live their lives disengaged from mainstream activities and values.

It was a week before the gathering was scheduled to begin and a relaxed but purposeful air of activity pervaded the camp. A number of people lounged in the river while a work party built a wooden booth that would serve as a welcome and information station for the hundreds of people expected to arrive during the Fourth of July weekend. The center of activity was a large circle of tepees, which gave the canyon meadow the appearance of a Native American village. Everyone acted as if the forest settlement were, in fact, their home. "Welcome home, brother," or "Welcome home, sister" was the greeting given to all new arrivals. Almost immediately, I began to offer this greeting as well.

Near the river a little dwelling had been constructed of willow sticks, bent and tied together to form a framework that looked like an upside-down bird's nest. Over this frame, blankets and tarps had been arranged to enclose the structure completely. The interior of this diminutive hut was dark. In the center of the earthen floor a shallow pit had been dug. Outside, a few feet away, a pile of smooth stones were roasting in the flames of a bonfire.

I joined a group of men who had congregated next to a large log near the little dwelling. I learned the structure was the community "sweat lodge." "There's room for one more," one of the men remarked, after I had expressed an interest in what they were doing. "Why don't you join us?"

I had never participated in a sweat lodge ceremony, but the men assured me I didn't need to know anything special ahead of time. So I joined the men, taking off my clothes and leaving them folded in a pile on top of the fallen log with the others'.

Inside the lodge, I sat naked on the ground with about a dozen men. After a few minutes, another man who was tending the bonfire carefully maneuvered several shovel loads of the heated stones into the central pit. Someone closed the entrance flap. One of the men began to chant and the rest of us joined him. The deep tones and rhythmic drone of our combined voices took my attention away from the discomfort of the crowded space. I felt a growing sense of camaraderie with the other men. The chanting stopped and the leader of the ceremony splashed water from an old coffee can onto the mound of hot stones in our midst. I had experienced steam baths and saunas in the past, but nothing had prepared me for the next few seconds.

An ominous hiss from the water, vaporizing as it hit the rocks, announced the searing cloud of live steam that assaulted my skin. My first thought was that someone had made a terrible mistake. Through some perverse irony I had come to this "healing" gathering to be scalded. Within moments I realized that my fears were unfounded; miraculously, I had not been burned. Another sharp hiss caused me to brace myself for the next torrid wave of steam. This second assault, although I could not have imagined it, was even more intense than the first. Every nerve ending in my skin was mobilized. If I could have bolted from that oven-like hut, I would have done so immediately. As it was I couldn't move, huddled on the darkened floor with the others.

This process—preparing for and then meeting wave after wave of scalding steam—continued for what seemed an interminable length of time. As the process developed, however, I found myself invigorated by it. I felt a genuine satisfaction in the accomplishment of enduring the heat. Finally, when I had given up hope that the ordeal would ever end, someone inside the tent shouted, "All my relations!" and the door-flap was thrown open to the fresh air. "All my relations!" is the traditional American Indian phrase used to end the sweat lodge ceremony. It is a simple declaration affirming man's relatedness to all living things.

Joining the other men from the sweat lodge, I ran the few steps to the river and plunged my super-heated body into the ice-cold water. The sensation was delicious. Splashing in the river with each other, we celebrated that special rapport of people who have shared a rite of passage. If there had been any doubt about it before, we were surely "brothers" now.

As I turned to get out of the water, I was startled by the sight of what appeared to be a moving carpet of bright yellow balls floating toward me in the stream. Was I hallucinating? No. Within moments the river was filled with them: hundreds of grapefruit. The grapefruit were being "herded" downstream by a contingent of "shepherds" who, with long sticks, kept their "flock" from straying onto the riverbank. The vision was startling: a sparkling clear river in the midst of a remote canyon wilderness and all of those bobbing, bright yellow grapefruit.

One of the shepherds informed me that a group of family members had caravanned to a citrus grove in Arizona and picked a truckload of fruit. Upon their return, they found a forest service road upstream from the group's campsite and devised this ingenious method to get the fruit into camp.

Maybe people can't live like this in the larger society, I thought to myself as I helped toss the grapefruit out of the stream. But at least it's a chance to be part of a community where people work together for the good of everyone, even if it's only for a week.

12

Sitting silently, doing nothing;
Spring comes, and the grass
grows by itself.

—*Zenerin*

IN A GRASSY CLEARING some distance from the main encampment, twenty people had formed what I had been told was a healing circle. I found an unobtrusive vantage point from which I could comfortably watch the group. Some of the healers were people I had seen engaged in other activities at the gathering. Now, however, they shared a communion of silence that was markedly different from the otherwise festive atmosphere that pervaded the camp. No one was speaking. Everyone was listening, it seemed, to the song of the birds and drone of the cicadas, to the hum of flying insects and the murmur of a little stream that ran nearby.

About ten minutes had elapsed when a bewildered man approached the clearing. He had great, dark circles under his eyes and a jaundiced cast to his skin. He walked with a shuffle and had a chaotic air about him, as if some unfathomable confusion had taken hold of his mind. Hesitantly, with tremendous strain in his voice, he announced, "I can't tell you why I am here!"

Well, I thought, this ought to be good. How in the world can these people do anything at all to help this man? He's not even willing or able to tell them what's wrong with himself.

A few minutes of silence passed. When the tension had almost reached the breaking point, a man with an eagle feather braided into his hair stood up and entered the circle. Seizing the distraught man with an intense gaze, the healer began to speak, the tone of his voice and the cadence of his words harmonizing with the sounds and tempo of the natural setting.

"Brother," he said softly, "whatever it is that has brought you here, we too have within us that same dis-ease. You serve only to reflect it. You have magnified it into what is for you an intolerable oppression."

The man whom the healer had addressed responded with a look of incomprehension. His glance roamed the circle restlessly, focusing dimly on each person seated on the grass. The healer answered the man's wordless plea. Once again the sound of the healer's voice filled the forest glade. "Each of us will look within ourselves and find the darkness that is the mirror of your pain. We'll find it here, inside!" he declared, touching the center of his own chest with his open palm. "And infuse it with the light of conscious love. Truly we, too, are afflicted with whatever it is that has brought you here today."

All the people closed their eyes. They began to rock back and forth, establishing a rhythm to the music of their inner selves. Encircled by healers, the distraught man sat down awkwardly, then slumped on the grass. Gradually the sound of everyone's breath became audible, creating a low hum. Individual chants rose in volume, blending into a harmony that joined with the drone of the cicadas. The sound grew to a pulsating force that filled the forest glade, surrounding the man who had come to this gathering to be healed.

The better part of an hour passed with the group rocking and chanting in this fashion. The sound finally diminished as, one by one, the healers ended their chant. The forest glade was quiet; only the natural sounds remained. I was surprised. A brighter look shone from the man's face. His agitation had lessened. He appeared to have come back to life.

Once again the healer addressed the man. "Brother," he said warmly, "as you walk through this camp, please know that each and every one of us carries the same disquiet that brought you to our midst. Whatever it is, thank you for bearing so well that burden for us all."

With that, the men and women sitting on the earth arose. Stepping forward, each one embraced this "brother" who had so laboriously found his way there. Perhaps it was the attention of or acceptance by the group, I conjectured, that was responsible for the change in the man. Whatever it was, his inner turmoil seemed to have eased considerably.

I found the process intriguing. Who could tell me what had transpired? I approached a tiny woman with raven black hair and sharply chiseled features. She was Ciana, a healer from Hawaii.

"What happened here?" I asked.

"I'll try to explain it to you," she answered. "First of all, you have to understand that words or explanations cannot really answer your question. What we are doing is beyond words. Some general information, though, might help to clarify the process. As you know, an overall harmony regulates the flow of life. The most obvious elements are the heartbeat and the pulse. The electrical rhythm in the brain and the rhythm of the breath are vital as well. Most of the dis-ease that people bring into our healing circle is characterized by a disturbance in one or another of these natural rhythms.

"Mystery schools and wisdom traditions teach that all of these so-called biorhythms are interrelated through a great harmony orchestrated by the breath," she continued. "By changing even slightly the breath's rhythm, the whole person is affected. If you wish, you can try it for yourself."

"How?" I asked.

"As you exhale count to seven," Ciana instructed. "Pause to the count of one at the end of your exhalation, then inhale to the count of seven. Pause once again to the count of one, then repeat the seven count during your next exhalation. Breathe in through your nose and out through your mouth. If you can establish this rhythm within yourself, you will harmonize with the principle of life that wishes only to conceive perfection from within itself. This rhythm is called 'The Mother's Breath,'" the healer explained. "I learned it from my teacher in Hawaii."

I sat back and began to breathe to the seven-count that Ciana had just prescribed. The only part of the woman's instruction that took an extra bit of concentration was the short pause between the inhalation and exhalation. I also had a tendency to pause for a longer period of time at the end of the exhalation, but within a few breaths I caught on. Ciana was right; I soon noticed a shift within myself. As I slowed and changed my breathing, I felt more at peace, more centered. I could feel a warm energy spreading throughout my body.

After a few minutes, she explained more. "When people are disturbed by egotism or emotions, their breathing becomes rhythmically uneven. From the earliest times, long before the advent of Western medicine, certain people observed this. These first practitioners discovered that, regardless of the nature of a person's anxiety, breath regulation could restore the fundamental harmony and sense of well-being inherent in each of us.

"Early healers also discovered sounds that could bring about balance or equilibrium. Over the course of many centuries, yogis in India catalogued various combinations of sounds which, when pronounced aloud, could modulate the breath's rhythm and affect our inner vibrations. Through this practice they learned to regulate the rhythm of the heart and other rhythms of the body. The result was a conscious orchestration of the harmony of the whole person. Today this is known as 'mantra-yoga.'

"Do you know how the resonance phenomenon in acoustics works?" Ciana asked.

"I learned about that recently," I replied, surprised to hear this technical term coming from a counterculture healer. "One of the scientists at the lab at UCLA where I work brought a couple of tuning forks into my workspace. The forks were tuned to the same pitch. When he struck one of them the sound from it started the other one vibrating. He said the effect was due to 'sympathetic vibration.'"

"That's precisely what we're trying to accomplish through our chants," Ciana replied. "The whole body is a living resonator. Every atom in it is affected by sound. Different vibrations affect the various organic systems. If we can harmonize 'sympathetically' with the person in the circle, we can affect his or her vibration. If we're in harmony with ourselves and with each other, then perhaps we can gently nudge someone's disharmony into a more harmonious state."

"Most of the physicists who work in psychological acoustics are concerned with environmental noise pollution and how it affects people in the workplace," I volunteered. "Oftentimes, these scientists are called in to a factory when productivity has declined and management can't find a reason for it. I don't know if the acousticians are ever called in to enhance a workspace."

"I don't know the answer to that either, but they should be," Ciana interjected. "Sound definitely can have a positive effect on the body. Music is a perfect example. It can either soothe or excite a person, and the whole body can be brought into harmony through it. In fact, Webster's definition of *health* is soundness of body.

"For thousands of years healers have depended on their observations of their patient's body rhythms. That's what modern doctors do with their stethoscopes and other monitoring devices. What we're doing here is trying to effect a change in those rhythms through non-intrusive means. We've got a lot going for us.

"First of all, a person who enters our circle has a high degree of motivation to re-establish a sense of harmony ... or he or she wouldn't be here in the first place. Just attending this gathering, walking miles through the mountains, is rejuvenating and balancing. Many of the people who come here live in cities where the energy is constricted: concrete poured over most of the earth, and relatively few living things to promote and maintain a natural balance. This is a healing gathering just by virtue of its location.

"A person's motivation is extremely important," Ciana continued. "If someone is aware that he or she is out of balance, and has the desire to be healthy, then the process naturally follows. All organisms have an inner wisdom that seeks balance and well-being. This includes human beings."

"With all the turmoil that mankind is creating on Earth, it wouldn't seem so," I said.

"But it's true," she replied. "On the physical level it's true. And on the esoteric level, perhaps you should let the higher beings decide what is working toward harmony. Let me finish answering your question, though," Ciana said.

"Another important element in this healing dynamic is the integrity of the healers themselves," she began. "By integrity, I mean the original sense of the word: wholeness. Every one of us has needed healing at one time or another." Ciana paused and smiled. It was a gentle, loving smile that reminded me of the expressions

I had seen on the faces of religious figures painted by the old masters. I wondered what had caused this sensitive and articulate woman to become a healer.

"We've all been wounded in one way or another and we carry the memory of that with us," she said, intimating my question. "In fact, it is usually some sort of personal trauma that initiates our work in the healing arts.

"Taking part in this work is a spiritual service for all of us. Ideally, during the ceremony we're not here at all. By that I mean our individual personalities aren't here. Our intention is to transcend our separate ego-selves so we may become a channel for the flow of a higher energy. I guess the closest way to describe this is to say we embody the energy of 'love.' It is this feeling from within that enables an outpouring of Spirit from us. But it's not Spirit, nor our chants, nor even a person's motivation that brings about healing," Ciana declared, seeming to negate all she'd just said.

"What is it then?" I asked.

"Real healing can take place only through a change in consciousness," Ciana answered. "Everything else is just therapy.

"All the spiritual traditions teach that each life is interconnected," she continued. "This healing technique is based on our belief that whatever we see is not only connected to, but a reflection of, ourselves. We reflect each other. People who come to this gathering seeking help only serve to reflect accentuated aspects of each and every one of us. Our process is analogous to looking in a mirror and seeing a smudge. The technique we're using to remove the smudge is to recognize that it's on our own face, rather than trying to polish it off the mirror. On a very fundamental level, it's accepting responsibility."

Together, Ciana and I smoked a pipe filled with sage and wild rose leaves that my new friend had gathered from the nearby hills. The fragrance of the smoke was light and delicate, reminding me of the smell of the summer blooms in the garden of my old house in Pennsylvania. Talking with Ciana had been illuminating. It seemed her ideas about breath and vibration, healing and harmony were directly related to my research of the old whistles. Perhaps the vessels had originally been used for healing. Certainly they had transformed me; I had become a different person. Ciana was correct in her assertion, the reason I had changed the direction of my life was that something in my mind had shifted. I had experienced a change in consciousness.

During the first few days of the festival, Michael-John and I spoke several times about the whistles. Now we both shared in the expectation of introducing them to the rest of the Rainbow Family. I was convinced that it was important to share the old instruments with them. These were the people who had returned to the land, embracing fundamental values and acknowledging a spiritual viewpoint. This gathering was the family's healing convocation. If the set of whistles could be used as a harmonic tool—a healing tool—certainly this was the group most likely to recognize and utilize it as such. The occasion I had been waiting for came on the night of the full moon.

Hundreds of feet above the river, on top of a mesa that formed one of the canyon walls, two separate groups had formed. Within an hour or so they would merge. Initially, however, one group had begun a lively celebration, while the other sat quietly some distance away. I was a member of the second group. About a hundred people sat on the ground in concentric rings spreading outward into the night. We could see the fire around which the other group had gathered. We could hear the muffled beat of their drums, but they were too far away for us to hear their voices. Although the moon was full, a line of high-flying clouds sporadically obscured the light, lending a mysterious air of expectancy to our silent assembly.

Two women who had traveled to the gathering from upstate New York distributed a candle and a small blue card to each person in our group. Within a few moments all the candles were lit, creating expanding rings of flickering lights. Reading by candlelight, everyone recited the invocation printed on the card:

> From the point of Light within the Mind of God
> Let Light stream forth into the minds of men.
> Let Light descend on Earth.
> From the point of Love within the Heart of God
> Let love stream forth into the hearts of men.
> May Christ return to Earth.
> From the centre where the Will of God is known
> Let purpose guide the little wills of men—
> The purpose, which the Masters know and serve.
> From the centre which we call the race of men
> Let the Plan of Love and Light work out.
> And may it seal the door where evil dwells.
> Let Light and Love and Power restore the
> Plan on Earth.[1]

A few moments of silence followed. Then Michael-John motioned me into the center of the group. I was sitting in one of the outer rings with the suitcase that contained the carefully wrapped artifacts. I made my way through several circles of people to the center, and distributed six of the seven whistles I had brought with me to the gathering.

Then I began my explanation. "These instruments were made by a highly evolved Indian people in South America ... five hundred years before Columbus was born. They are still considered sacred objects by the descendants of the people who made them."

Reaching down to the ground I grasped a handful of dusty soil. Then I raised my hand over my head and released the dirt. As dust slowly cascaded from my hand, I solemnly proclaimed, "In those times, a man's sworn oath was to grasp a handful of earth and look toward the sun. By so doing, he invoked the very foundation of his existence. This vessel," I declared, holding up the earthenware artifact that had started me out on my quest, "was made by a people with that understanding."

As I spoke, I felt as if a spirit of transcendent expression had taken over my speech. I had not rehearsed what I was going to say, but sitting under the stars on this remote mesa in southern New Mexico, and the group itself, elicited my impassioned explanation.

In a rhythmic voice, I intoned hopeful words about the rebirth of the ideas embodied in the ancient instruments. I spoke about the possibility for the reemergence and manifestation of those ideas through the actions and lives of the members of our family. I spoke about the renewal of a spiritual understanding in America, a land seemingly overcome with material concerns, and yet at the same time, a country that still held the essential creed of One Nation Under God. I declared that we were a congregation of this reawakening, and our gathering was a concrete statement of our collective vision for a harmonious world. More than a hundred people listened to me in silence.

As I spoke, I saw myself emerging as a leader of this group, another spiritual focalizer like Michael-John. Suddenly, in the middle of a sentence, it dawned on me that I was, in effect, talking to myself. My role was just that, a role—assumed and not real. The words and ideas, the vision and the hope, were what I most needed to hear and to believe. I had come to this gathering with full-blown egotism to share the power of my discovery and take my place as a leader without the humility that an authentic leader would embody. Now, for the first time, I saw my pretense. Even more so, I deeply felt my own need for the love and support of these people, and for their acceptance. I was humbled.

As I continued to speak, my voice softened, and my eyes looked down to the earth at my feet for the remainder of the ceremony. Finally, with the passing of the clouds, the moon appeared full. I handed my original vessel to someone in the group and, using the moment of light, I quietly instructed the people with whistles how to play them. Then they began to harmonize, creating the haunting chant that had led me to this place and to this moment of truth.

As the sounds of the old whistles combined, a perceptible ripple of awareness traveled through the family. Within a few minutes people began to come forward. They quietly switched places with those holding instruments in the inner circle. Thus, everyone who wished to was able to play. This went on for some time, the voice of the combined whistles sustained by many breaths.

I sat very still, focusing on my inner experience. I had uncovered a hidden aspect of myself. I sensed a healing of my pretense. I was accepted, even welcomed into this group of people, and I could feel their love and support flowing toward me as I stood in the center of their circle. In and of itself, their acceptance was healing. A vision of the black snake that had appeared at Healing Waters on the solstice crossed my mind, and I thought of the man who had entered the circle of healers. Then I knew the truth: I was that bewildered man, stumbling into the healing circle, being received and being transformed.

13

Someday, after we have mastered the winds, the waves, the tides and gravity, we shall harness for God the energies of love. Then for the second time in the history of the world man will have discovered fire.

—*Pierre Teilhard de Chardin*

As I drove back to Los Angeles, I felt a sense of belonging I hadn't known before. I'd never had the feeling of belonging to any group, neither as a teenager nor in college. But now I was a member of the Rainbow Family. On the day following the meditation on the mesa, several healers had approached me to ask about the whistles. When they learned I was preparing to make the whistles, all the healers expressed interest in having a set for their "branch" of the family. Now I had even more incentive to complete my work with George Binkele.

While I was figuring out the final dimensions for the resonance cavities, Binkele was sculpting a new model of the vessel I had purchased at the auction in Pennsylvania. Across a span of centuries and despite the vast cultural differences, its simple design conveyed a universal message. The contemplative expression of the figural Indian implied meditation or introspection, and the object that he clasped in his hands appeared to be a stylized version of the modeled seashell that formed the spouted chamber of the artifact. A person holding the instrument was in part assuming the Indian's posture. Since the figure holding the shell was a vessel for human breath, so might a person playing the instrument see himself as a vessel, and an instrument for the breath of the Divine.

Binkele and I decided to make a replica of the whistle rather than work from the original. Casting a mold from the old artifact was risky and, due to shrinkage in the clay, would result in a slightly smaller version than the original. I was determined to produce exact reproductions. It was well into the fall of 1977 before we completed the production molds. In the midst of the process, I cast a vessel from the master molds to see if all the pieces fit together before we committed ourselves to the final design. The pieces fit perfectly. There on the workbench in front of me was an exact replica of an earthenware whistle made by a Chimú potter nearly a thousand years before. With Mr. Binkele's help, I had realized my dream.

When the molds were completed I moved them to California Design Works in Marina del Rey. Besides directing me to Mr. Binkele, Marty Steinbrecher, the owner of this pottery manufacturing company, had agreed to rent me space in his shop when I was ready to make vessels. Marty's factory was nearly the exact opposite of the Santa Monica Mold Shop. Whereas Binkele's workshop was small, quiet, and filled with little carvings, my new place of work was a cavernous, barnlike building, harboring several gas-fired kilns that roared continuously throughout the day. A radio, perpetually tuned to a Spanish broadcasting station, was nearly successful in competing with the overall din. Within this factory, an energetic contingent of Mexican workers cast an extraordinarily diverse variety of hookahs or water pipes. These artistically designed

but quasi-legal implements were used by people to smoke mari-
juana, hashish, or some other mind-altering substance. Perhaps
it was some sort of cosmic irony, I thought, for me to be making vessels into which people would blow their breaths for meditation in
a factory that was producing smoking pipes through which people would draw in their breaths to get "stoned." After a short time,
I decided the best place for me was outside, in the factory's backyard. It was quieter there, and the air was free of the dust parti-
cles that clouded the building.

Although I had assembled several vessels from the master molds
in Mr. Binkele's shop, making more than one instrument at a time
was an entirely different proposition. Making several vessels in a day
was downright daunting. The main difficulty once again was with
the little resonance cavity. To cast and fine-tune each cavity was a
meticulous and painstaking operation; experience taught me that
I needed to produce at least a half-dozen cavities for every instrument I actually assembled. Each vessel required a custom fit and
an absolutely precise alignment of the whistle cavity with the air
stream. If the alignment was incorrect, the fragile sphere had to be
removed from its concave seat on the back of the Indian's head.
Invariably, the resonance cavity was destroyed in the process.

A second problem arose after the whistle was attached. Fabricating the bridge handle that surrounded and enclosed the resonance cavity was a delicate procedure; one false move could
dislodge the whistle and render it useless. Gradually I learned.
The color of the factory slip was stark white, and I explored a number of techniques to achieve a more natural appearance to the
completed instruments. I painted colored slip onto the finished
vessels, experimented with numerous dyes and stains, and even
tried a brown glaze. The glaze was the worst approach, creating a
barrier of glass between the earthenware and the environment. I
discovered that by adding iron oxide and cobalt to the slip the

clay became earthen brown. This gave the instruments a soft, organic feeling, pleasing to look at and inviting to hold.

Another problem arose in drying the completed castings. The bridge was thicker than the spouted and figural chambers. Consequently, this thicker section dried at a slower rate than the rest of the vessel. To avoid distortion while drying, I developed a procedure to dehydrate each vessel very slowly. I accomplished this by covering the unfired pottery with thin plastic sheeting that inhibited the rapid evaporation of the water in the clay. Several times each day I would turn the plastic to release a little of the condensation. This drying process took about a week, but ensured uniform shrinkage of the assembled instrument.

Experimenting with the color, mixing the clay, tuning the resonance cavities, assembling and then drying and firing each vessel required an enormous amount of time and attention. Week after week I would arrive at the factory before eight in the morning and remain until after dark. Finally the first sets of instruments began to emerge from the kiln, each vessel tuned to a different pitch. By playing two instruments simultaneously I could listen to the difference tone produced by the combined sounds, then choose the pair that created the best effect. My choice was subjective, but I knew what I was listening for. If contiguous whistles were pitched too widely apart, they produced what I considered to be an abrasive sound. If they were pitched too closely together, the beat was barely perceptible. When I wanted to play more than two vessels at a time I would enlist the help of the Mexican workers. During their coffee or lunch break we would stand around in the backyard near my workbench and try out various combinations. I tried to explain to the men that the whistles were intended for meditation, but I'm not sure they ever really knew why I was making them. Nevertheless, the men seemed to enjoy playing the instruments.

Every morning the men would greet me, "Buenos Días, señor—
¿Cómo está usted?"

"Bien bien, muy bien," I would reply. "¿Qué pasa, amigo?"

"Trabajando mucho, amigo. Trabajando mucho."

This was the extent of my Spanish vocabulary. Making these
vessels was "much work" for me as well. As I assembled and shipped
completed sets of instruments, I felt another level of tension within
me relax—an inner acknowledgment that indeed I had reached
my goal.

By this time I had decided I could not sell sets of instruments.
The vessels were spiritual tools. I felt their integrity was best expressed by gifting them to people who were deeply drawn to them,
and I didn't need the money. My share of the proceeds from the
sale of my grandfather's machine shop still provided enough in-
come to satisfy my financial needs.

For the most part I sent completed sets of whistles to people
who had a deep desire to explore them further. It was a diverse
group, from research scientists at universities to Rainbow Family
members. I imagined that through this broad spectrum of people an understanding of the vessels' original purpose might be
revealed. But that was a secondary consideration. In and of themselves the whistles were valuable as inspirational tools.

When I developed a more natural color or added a new design,
I would update the earlier sets with the newer edition, retrieving
the previous versions whenever possible. I would break the whistles
sent back to me and return the shattered pieces to the earth. Mr.
Binkele eventually completed the molds for an additional three
figures. One by one, I incorporated the three new figures into my
work.

The recipients were sincere in their interest. Often, from their
farm or spiritual community, they would either bring or mail to
me some earth or a small bottle of water, asking that I add it to

the clay I would be using to make their set of instruments. One woman gave me sand from Ayers Rock in Australia. Another sent me some of the ash that her guru, Sai Baba, supposedly manifested out of thin air. I received water from a glacier in Montana, copal from Guatemala, and frankincense from Europe, as well as feathers from a variety of birds. A shaman brought me the dried carcass of a bat. All of these elements I mixed into the clay or placed within the completed vessels before firing them.

The factory slip from which I made the whistles was a mixture of clays gathered from California, Kentucky, and Tennessee. These clays were then mixed with water piped to Los Angeles from the Colorado River. As I became aware of the geographic diversity of these elements, I began to envision the playing of the whistles as a means to call forth the telluric forces from a vast area of North America. They were indeed a means to animate the earth.

I augmented these forces with rainwater I collected in buckets and a drop of water from the Pacific Ocean. Water that came directly from the environment was surely in better balance than water that had been treated with chemicals or enclosed in a plastic pipe. That balance, I thought, might become a part of my instruments as well.

My alchemy began on a visit to Esalen. Walking along Pfeiffer Beach near Big Sur, I was drawn to a huge rock protruding from the ocean about fifty yards off shore. In the center of the boulder was an opening through which waves periodically crashed, sending a cascading spray of water into the air. As I watched wave after wave break against the rock, I felt as if I were standing at a visible juncture where the primary elements of my clay met in their most vital interplay. This was the place where the ocean stopped and the earth began. Here, embodied in this implacable stone, was the palpable point where the earth had yielded to the relentless movement of the sea.

I had a sudden desire to bring some of that airborne spray back to Los Angeles to add to my clay. Taking off my clothes, I waded out to the boulder with an empty bottle and caught what I could of the spray as the waves crashed through the rock. I was able to catch only a little water with each wave. So I stood there for twenty minutes or so, naked and holding the bottle up in the air.

For a moment I wondered what I would say if asked by a park ranger to explain what I was doing. But no one showed up. I got back to the beach without incident, put on my clothes and returned to Los Angeles with a small container of the captured spray. When I got back to the shop, I mixed a droplet of sea water into each batch of clay, empowering my instruments with both the strength and compromise of that power point.

The final ingredients I added to my clay formula were pulverized bits of seashell. I had learned that the shell portrayed on my original whistle was that of a *Spondylus* or thorny oyster, a mollusk that inhabits the deep Pacific waters off the Ecuadorian coast. Found at ceremonial centers and incorporated as a design element in pre-Columbian art, the thorny oyster had been imported to Peru from the earliest times and remained significant up to the time of the conquest. A Spanish chronicler reported that the court of the Chimú king had included an attendant known as "The Preparer of the Way." This man's function was to walk before his monarch, scattering the pulverized dust of Spondylus shells in the king's path.

Symbolically, seashells represent the completion of life. I imagined that with every step he took, the Chimú king was reminded to consider his actions in light of his own mortality. Perhaps the shell depicted on my Chimú whistle was meant to convey that the artifact itself was a shell: a remnant of another man's life, the container for another man's breath, perhaps the instrument for another man's soul-search.

I bought a Spondylus shell at a seashell shop in Malibu and added crushed bits of it to my clay. This calcified shadow of watery life would add its energy to my pottery as well.

At the time this alchemy seemed reasonable. I was a metaphysician, or at least a metaphysician in training. In retrospect, however, I was following a recipe without knowing what I was creating, adding alchemical ingredients like spices to my original insight. Inherent in this alchemy was my continuing search for something more. Although the primary focus of my inner work was to open my heart and transform that dark aspect I had glimpsed of myself, I still longed for companionship and a meaningful relationship. I had had several opportunities for a loving relationship, but in each instance I had failed to sustain the deep connection I wished to have in my life.

As my hands worked in the clay, I replayed in my mind a series of failed relationships. Traveling with the whistles afforded me ample opportunity to meet potential partners. Invariably, though, I would choose someone with whom I was unable to sustain the connection. Initially I thought my inability to establish a lasting relationship was simply because of my divorce. I was not yet ready for anything long term. Through my choice of inappropriate partners, I ensured against making a real-world commitment. Besides, my self-image as a wandering shaman and my mission with the whistles precluded my settling down to a conventional relationship. At any moment, I might be called to Egypt to play the old instruments in a Pharaoh's tomb or to uncover yet another mystery.

Still, I was unable to explain my attraction to relationships that with tiresome surety held the promise, through their inevitable endings, for great emotional upheaval. Why, time and again, did I put myself in a position to experience such deep disappointment?

One psychological theory provided a possible explanation. According to Dr. Grof, any unusual trauma from birth or early childhood is remembered on the deepest level of the psyche. In an effort to somehow resolve this early trauma, a person may be drawn to a situation that evokes the very same feelings associated with their initial childhood terror.

I found a clue to my afflicted pattern in two incidents that occurred when I was three years old. The first incident occurred on an afternoon in late June when I strayed from my house to a nearby construction site. Finding a hole in the ground filled with muddy water, I began to stir the water with a stick. I slipped and fell into the hole. My mouth was under water. Standing on my toes I was just barely able to breathe through my nose. I felt abandoned, and I was terrified. I thought I was going to die. I tried to climb out of the hole, but the wet earthen walls were slick with mud and I slipped back. Again and again I tried, but I failed. Then, in an instant, I found myself standing on solid ground a few feet away from the water-filled hole. Dripping muddy water, I walked home to find my father (my mother was in the hospital having my baby sister). My dad washed the mud off me with an outdoor hose. I don't think I told him what had occurred. To this day I still don't know how I got out of that hole.

The second incident happened that same summer. Early one evening, I awoke in my bed to find that the babysitter to whom I had been entrusted had disappeared. I was alone. With increasing terror and a sickening feeling of fear that I had been abandoned, I searched the empty house looking for someone. Still in my pajamas, I ran out of the house and then down the sidewalk until I found someone (perhaps the babysitter) who brought me home.

Indelibly etched in my mind was my primal terror, rooted in a fear of abandonment. In an effort to somehow resolve this core anxiety, I was drawn to create situations in my adult relationships that would precipitate a similar level of emotional distress. It was my way of bringing my deepest childhood fears to the surface in an effort to resolve them. I tried a variety of approaches: affirmations, neuro-linguistic programming, as well as highly focused self-awareness. Nothing helped; I continued to initiate relationships with eventual painful endings.

I imagined my pottery as a more active means for transforming my self-destructive pattern. Over and over, I worked my anguished feelings from each failed relationship into an earthen form that sounded forth a clear note. Then I fired each vessel to a white-hot ember while incinerating in my mind the pain I had worked into my clay.

Beyond fabricating the whistles, playing them with groups of people offered me another avenue for shifting my patterns and learning to love. No one was prepared for what happened when the whistles stopped. Plunged quite suddenly into the absolute still-ness of essential being, everyone's question of purpose and mean-ing dissolved into a quiet pool of thought-free equanimity. After several minutes of silence, I would conclude each meditation with a prayer: "Dear Lord God, who lives within us as our essential self, grant that this service be one expression of thy deepest love." Invariably, in the warm silence that followed, a meeting of unveiled eyes would initiate the longed-for connection. I experienced many such moments: in the forested, star-lit Sierras; in a converted aviary in Topanga Canyon, and in the meditation hall of a hacienda on the edge of the Rio Grande in Albuquerque, New Mexico. Though I'd yet to sustain such intimacy with one special partner, at least I was learning how to open my heart to love.

14

For having come so far through
flesh and cells in darkness,
for being the mysterious
stranger and the one whom
the mysterious stranger
affrights, we stand on this
enchanted evening bathed in
a richness even the gods
can not imagine—and with
no other clue in the darkness.

—*Richard Grossinger*

W ITH RELENTLESS DETERMINATION and what seemed an all-consuming effort, I produced sixty-four sets of instruments (seven per set) in less than a year. To do this, I cast at least a thousand vessels and their attendant whistle cavities. It's all I did: I ate, I slept, I made vessels. In the process, I mastered the ceramic techniques necessary to reproduce the old artifacts. With the completion of the sixty-fourth set, I was ready to leave Los Angeles. The noise, chaotic traffic, and polluted air in the city had become more and more oppressive. It was time to move on.

In May 1978 I visited the Southwest and found myself drawn to the mountains of northern New Mexico. I felt invigorated and uplifted by the altitude and fresh air of the high desert. Wind-eroded buttes rose like modern sculptures from the brick-red earth into a turquoise-blue sky. The aspen- and pine-covered mountains beckoned with warm invitation. The New Mexico landscape was spacious, a vastness punctuated by cozy clusters of adobe homes with enormous woodpiles and outdoor ovens. I wondered if I could learn from the ancient pottery tradition that still flourished in the area.

Through a mutual friend I met Ray and Barbara Stevens, who had left city life to build an adobe home and raise their family in Chimayo, New Mexico. Chimayo was predominantly a Hispanic community located about forty-five minutes north of Santa Fe. I spent an evening with Ray and Barbara, swapping stories in their rustic kitchen. Before I left New Mexico, my new friends had agreed to find a place in their community for me to live.

About a month later in Los Angeles, I drove downtown to San Pedro Street for some sushi. I was disappointed. A sign in the window announced that my favorite restaurant was closed. I didn't have a second choice, so I wandered around the neighborhood looking for another possibility. I passed up a few sushi bars until I saw a sign for a restaurant located in the basement of a modern bank building. It was not at all the sort of restaurant I would normally be drawn to. For some reason, though, I entered the modern building and took the elevator to the underground level where the posh Japanese restaurant was located.

The well-dressed businessman seated next to me at the polished wooden bar was an aficionado of sushi. "The Spanish mackerel is especially good this evening," Richard Kandarian suggested, after we had introduced ourselves. "I eat here whenever I'm in Los Angeles," he declared. "This is the best sushi in southern California. We don't have many sushi bars in Detroit," he added. "I'm flying home tomorrow."

"Detroit is pretty far from the ocean," I agreed. "I usually eat at a restaurant around the corner, but for some reason it's closed tonight. This is my first time here."

"Well, you're in luck," Mr. Kandarian stated. "You've stumbled into the best sushi bar in L.A."

The gregarious businessman was right. It was the best sushi I had ever eaten. I tried a number of dishes for the first time and discovered Chawan-Mushi, a hot egg custard containing tantalizing bits of baked shrimp and scallops along with a boiled ginkgo nut. Everything was delicious. Toward the end of the dinner, I mentioned my upcoming move to Mr. Kandarian. "I'm going to miss eating sushi when I leave California," I remarked.

"Where are you going?" he asked.

"I'm trying to find a place to live near Santa Fe, New Mexico," I replied. "It's the capital city," I added, as a way to more specifically identify what I presumed might be an obscure area of the country. After all, I was talking to an international businessman from Detroit who was in transit from the Far East. "So far I haven't had much luck," I continued. "I have some friends there, though, who are looking for me. I'm hopeful something will turn up."

"That's interesting," Mr. Kandarian exclaimed. "My brother has a cabin in the mountains north of Santa Fe. If you haven't already lived there, it's a place you've probably never heard of. Chimayo."

The light in the room seemed to change to a surreal yellow-orange, and I caught the flash of a feathered wing out of the corner of my eye. I wasn't hallucinating. Knowing about cosmic-docking operations still doesn't prepare you for them. As it turned out, the cabin was available, and Mr. Kandarian's brother, Bob, agreed to rent it to me. The cabin was less than a fifteen-minute drive from the home of my new friends, the Stevens family.

I rented the cabin over the phone without even seeing it. As I drove away from California I wondered how fate was working to arrange the details of my life. The next afternoon, as I eased my car and heavily laden trailer down a precipitous driveway leading into what seemed a remote and uninhabited canyon, I wondered if I had made a mistake. It was my only moment of doubt in the two years I lived there.

The cabin was actually a converted mobile home. Bob Kandarian, a nuclear engineer employed at the nearby Los Alamos National Laboratories, had dragged the dwelling more than a mile down a dirt road to a little meadow situated in the bottom of the canyon. My landlord had sided the dwelling with cedar planks and added a sturdy porch with a hanging swing to face the pond, which he had dug on the property. A few steps from the cabin's door, a narrow stream passed by on its winding course through the canyon meadow.

I soon learned that the little stream that flowed through the canyon was really a river, and a very special river at that. In another part of the country the Frijoles River would be considered a brook, but in New Mexico, where water is a precious commodity, a stream that flows year-round is called a river. My new home was the first human habitation the Rio Frijoles reached on its journey from the mountainous snow pack to the Rio Grande. A few miles downstream, the river meandered past the area's most sacred shrine, the Santuario de Chimayo.

The Santuario is a Catholic Church built in 1813 on a site long considered sacred by the local Pueblo Indians. For centuries, Native Americans have attributed an extraordinary healing virtue to the earth in the vicinity of the Santuario. The healing tradition has been continued within the church. Each day, in a tiny room next to the chapel, pilgrims—some of whom come from great distances—remove handfuls of the treasured dirt. In an adjoining room, crutches and canes bear silent witness to cures effected on the spot. Miraculously, it is said, the hole in the earth refills itself each night in order to provide more of the healing dirt for the next day's arrivals.

The old logging road that led to Mr. Kandarian's property continued for about a mile past my cabin until it turned into a trail at the edge of the Pecos Wilderness. Each day was a new adventure for my beloved Whippet dog, Key-Z, and me to walk up the road and into the forest. I bought a book on wildlife in New Mexico and identified Indian Paintbrush as the plant that gave a red splash of color to the ground. Cholla was the cactus Key-Z and I had to steer clear of. I discovered pieces of mica that flaked apart like little windowpanes. After a rainstorm I marveled at the tiny flowers that appeared, as if by magic, from nowhere.

The pond on the east side of the cabin provided a liquid reflection of the dark green pines and warm earth colors of my new home. Huge Ponderosas with great black scars in their bark gave evidence to an ancient fire. Cedars and the smaller Piñon Pines seemed to squat against the hills like old men wearing ponchos in the rain. In the mornings I would sit on the porch swing with a cup of coffee and watch the sunrise over the mountains. First light brought the earth to life. Grey shadows turned to rich, pink hues as the hillsides warmed in the sunlight. Now and then the stillness of the morning was broken with a splash, and occasionally I caught a shimmering glimpse from a trout in the midst of its leap.

In the late afternoon, before sunset, my private theater hosted an airborne ballet as a flock of swallows circled above the pond. The birds would swoop and glide, turning seamless figure-8s before skimming the water with beaks open to capture some of the precious liquid. I would hike up to the canyon rim and watch the azure sky turn purple as the sun sank behind the western wall of the Jemez range. The night sky was alight with thousands of stars, and I began to sleep outside beside the riverbank. Before closing my eyes, I would sometimes see for a brief instant the fiery trail of a meteor as it flashed across the vaulted dome above me. The ever-changing murmur of the stream, splashing over the rocks, lulled me to sleep. Occasionally I would hear the yip and howl from a pack of coyotes on some distant hill.

As a boy I had not spent much time outside of a city or suburban environment. I had explored the woods and fields near my house in Wilmington, gone on a few overnight hikes with the Boy Scouts, and once or twice camped out in an old Army tent in my back yard. That was the extent of my experience. Now I virtually lived outdoors. The only time I brought my sleeping bag into the cabin was when it rained.

I set up my workbench on the cabin porch, and, first thing each morning, I would pour clay into one set of molds. After breakfast, I prepared the molds for a second vessel and then began to assemble the first instrument of the day. The quiet of the mountains made it easier for me to tune each whistle, but the dry climate necessitated a new, critical timing in my work. If I cast more than one vessel at a time, the second instrument would dry to an unworkable condition before I could get around to taking it out of its mold. The orchestration of my movements became a kind of pottery dance, a T'ai Chi with clay that flowed like the nearby river, synchronized with the overall harmony of the environment. Invariably, whenever I was out of sorts with myself, I would struggle with each vessel and destroy it.

After lunch I walked into the mountains. I developed the habit of carrying a plastic sack to collect whatever trash I chanced to find along the way. In the past, local residents had used this outlying area as a dump, strewing refuse everywhere. Cleaning up the canyon and the surrounding hillsides became my avocation. Thousands of cans and bottles littered the landscape, but within a few years, I thought, the land could be returned to its natural state.

I saw the irony in spending most of each day constructing two clay bottles and the rest of my time picking up the discarded containers. Many of the jars and cans were filled with sediment, and I would empty them to return the trapped earth to the land. I visualized the whole area as a network of energies that had adjusted to the intrusion of the debris. By removing these foreign bodies, I was restoring the land. As I filled my sack with glass, plastic, and tin, I began to sense a sympathetic respiration from my new home. I was a part of this land, and my function was to scour the area for anything that interfered with the well-being and harmony of the whole.

The months slipped past the year mark. To my eyes the valley grew more and more radiant. I was being nurtured by this place. As time went by, I recognized that my effort to bring the environment into better balance was an exterior manifestation of my continuing effort to restore wholeness within myself. The land and I were healing each other.

I visited several Pueblo Indian ruins in the nearby Española Valley. As I walked amidst the adobe ruins of the area's first inhabitants, I noticed the contrast between their tribal culture and the high civilizations of the Andes. The Indians of the Southwest had constructed their dwellings of mud or small rocks. They had not built anything that even approached the grandeur of what I had seen in South America, but the early people who had lived here had been potters too.

Here and there, nestled in a rocky crevice or exposed on top of the ground, I discovered clay shards from earthenware vessels made by native potters before Christopher Columbus reached the New World. I picked up one of the shards and sensed a feeling from it. Once again I had found the calcified memory of an ancient people. Contained within the bit of broken pottery was a song that might have been a prayer to the earth. Although the words were now lost in the gentle breeze that blew across the deserted mesa, somehow the essential human message remained.

I pulverized the little relic and added the ancient pottery dust to my clay. My hope was that the old Indian prayer might be reborn and ring forth once again with the sound of the whistles. If the old spirits were still in Peru, as the Indian in Cuzco had informed me, then undoubtedly they were in New Mexico as well.

Each day I sat at my workbench and assembled two clay instruments. My work became my meditation, and I began to see it as something other than a pottery dance, or a mission to revive a valuable tool for the exploration of consciousness. What I was really doing, I finally grasped, was working on myself. The clarity of sound that I sought to achieve from each instrument was my continuing search for clarity within myself.

In assembling the front and rear sections of each whistle, I needed to carve an opening into the rear section where the spouted, bottle-like chamber would be joined to the figural Indian's back. This was the connecting passageway between the two sections of the vessel through which a person's breath would flow before activating the whistle and emanating into the world as a sound.

From the very beginning, as I was learning to make the instruments, I carved this opening in the shape of a heart. This heart-shaped passageway was not a feature of the originals; it was my secret signature destined for discovery only when and if a vessel should be broken. There amidst the pieces, to offset that destructive moment of shattered pottery, in whatever place or circumstance, the message I had put inside the bottle would be revealed: a secret heart carved in the clay.

According to Sufi wisdom tradition, the essential medium that underlies verbal communication is the breath through which our words are formed. In the same manner as speech, the sound that rings forth from each vessel is also carried on its player's breath. As a person's breath passes through the clay, it is guided into form by the heart shape within each vessel. As I traveled what I initially thought to be an ancient and mysterious byway, I found the opening of my heart was really the crux of my journey. My ardent hope was that the whistles would serve to open other people's hearts as well.

We all live within the ruins of an ancient
structure whose vast size has hitherto rendered
it invisible.

—*John Michell*

IN THE WINTER OF MY SECOND YEAR in New Mexico, I headed
for the center of the Inca Empire once again. This time I brought
a set of replica whistles. I planned two stopovers: one in Mexico
City and the other in Quito, Ecuador. My stopover in Mexico was
to meet with a group of people who were exploring the country's
archaeological ruins in search of spiritual remnants and still-active
energy channels among the stones. Our plan was to travel together
for several days, playing the replica whistles at various sites. We
believed the sound might catalyze the subtle energies discerned
and brought into form by pre-Columbian architects.

Ever since reading John Michell's book, *The View Over Atlantis*,[1]
I had been fascinated with the concept that in ancient times people were knowledgeable in a mysterious art or science that enabled
them to perceive telluric and cosmic energies. The idea that ancient edifices and prehistoric temples had been sited and built to
utilize these subtle energies implied a profound understanding
of an important body of knowledge that for the most part seemed

to have been lost or forgotten in our times.

During the second half of the twentieth century, interest in this subject has been rekindled, however, and groups have formed to explore the mysteries. Westerners, convinced of the efficacy of acupuncture, study the old Chinese system of geomancy, which was used to site cities and temples in China. In Great Britain thousands of people regularly trudge the countryside in search of alignments thought to connect various prehistoric sites and power grids across the planet. Throughout the Americas people congregate at special mounds, pyramids, and ceremonial centers to meditate or pray. I was excited to be joining the exploration.

I met Robert Mann and Yati at the airport in Mexico City. Yati was a vibrant sixty-year-old woman from Holland who had moved to Mexico twenty years earlier to teach at a Montessori school. Robert was in his thirties, a Canadian national who taught English at the language school in Cuernavaca. I had met Robert the previous summer during a whistle session at the School of American Research in Santa Fe. After playing the vessels, Robert had introduced himself as a member of a metaphysical group. In the course of our conversation he asked about the possibility of my bringing the whistles to Mexico to play with his friends in the ancient ruins they explored regularly. I had an intuition that playing the whistles with Robert and his friends in Mexico would be important.

The first stop of our exploration was to be the temple at Tepoztlán.

"Where is Tepoztlán?" I asked, as the three of us drove south from the capital in Robert's white Econoline van.

"Tepoztlán is a village a few miles from Cuernavaca," Robert answered. "In 1895 a Toltec temple was discovered on the top of a cliff that overlooks the town. The old ruin is not an important tourist site so it's usually abandoned. The village *brujos*, the healers, still perform ceremonies there. We'll get a good night's sleep and then meet the others in the morning before we hike up to the temple."

I spent the night at a small, well-tended hacienda on the outskirts of Tepoztlán where I met the others with whom I would be traveling. In addition to Robert and Yati, a young couple from France would be traveling with us, along with Rosa, a middle-aged woman of Mexican/Indian descent, and three other women. Nine of us would be exploring the ruins, more than enough to play all of the whistles.

The next morning, as we followed the trail that led to the temple, I hiked beside Yati. "That's *tolache,*" she said, pointing to a leafy plant growing alongside the path. "It's a well-known herb here. The local women sometimes put it in their men's coffee to make them *tonto*—that's foolish, or stupid—and easily managed. But the herb is dangerous. An extra large dose has been known to cause idiocy."

"How did you learn about herbs?" I asked.

"A local woman, a *bruja,* taught me," Yati answered. "She's my neighbor. Sometimes when we walk together my friend will point out a plant and explain how it's used here. How did you learn about the whistles?" Yati asked.

I told her a brief version of my story.

"Do you know about the legend of an acoustical 'key'?" my hiking companion asked, glancing over at me. Yati was a gray-haired woman with piercing blue eyes who spoke English with a trace of a Dutch accent. "The legend foretells that one day a certain sound will unlock an ancient door that leads into an altogether different reality ... a different dimension," she added.

"I haven't heard about an acoustical 'key,'" I answered, "although I have read that in ancient times special priests in Mexico and South America were reputed to be 'scientists' of sound. Supposedly they could cut large stones along precise harmonic lines and then resonate them into position."

"That's a superficial manifestation," Yati retorted, as though dismissing my esoteric gossip with a shrug of her shoulders. "The pyramids are just an outward form to draw our attention to a special place. What I am referring to is the 'spherical' dimension, the dimension that spans duality.

"The ruins aren't really important in themselves," she continued, "except for the fact that they draw us to a location where the old masters discerned an energy fluctuation that affects consciousness. As dense as we've become," she laughed, "if we didn't stumble upon a huge pile of rocks on the ground—and neatly arranged at that—we'd never discover the energy on our own."

"I've never heard the pyramids described as a 'neatly arranged pile of rocks,'" I replied. "From what I've read, they're much more than that. Archaeo-astronomers have discovered that many of the megalithic constructions were precisely oriented toward certain stars or stellar events. Pyramid geometry reflects sophisticated mathematical formulas that modern people are just beginning to decipher with computer technology."

"The megaliths aren't problems that can be solved with computers or slide rules," Yati answered disdainfully. "They're mysteries! Mysteries don't always exist to be solved. In fact, much of the value in megalithic architecture is their mysteriousness. Even if measurements prove that the pyramids line up with each other, or the Pleiades, or Detroit, that's not the point. The ancient megaliths present us with an opportunity to go beyond the problem-solving mentality, to explore the deep unknown. Quantitative measurements and geometrical considerations will always be a secondary feature of something much more basic—much deeper—and that is the monument's ability to catalyze consciousness."

"Is the spherical dimension a level of consciousness that can explain the miracles magicians supposedly were able to perform?" I asked.

"There aren't any miracles," Yati answered. "What we categorize as a miracle is only an event or a phenomenon we don't understand. The only miracle is the moment of recognition when nothing is 'other' any longer. I call it the 'phenomenal' moment when the illusion of separation maintained by the ego finally dissolves.

"Getting back to your whistles, though. I suspect that they may, in fact, be part of a global mystery that is connected to the megalithic constructions," she continued. "Whoever built the pyramids certainly didn't leave the key to their secret buried under their doorstep."

"How do you think it fits together?" I asked. I felt a bit confused by the woman's direct, no-nonsense approach that somehow seemed in contrast to her metaphysical speculations.

"Obviously a superior intelligence constructed the pyramids," Yati answered. "And I think that many of the monuments, although in different parts of the world, were all built by the same beings."

"By the same beings!" I exclaimed. I stopped walking for a moment to catch my breath. "Who do you think built the pyramids, visitors from outer space?"

"Don't be ridiculous," the woman retorted. "People constructed them. But I don't believe the ideas inherent in their design originated with what we know today as human intelligence. What I'm getting at is, If a secret is yet to be discovered in, say, the Great Pyramid in Egypt, and it is an acoustical key that will ultimately reveal that secret, then perhaps the builders consciously concealed the necessary sound on the other side of the world—here in the Americas for instance. Your whistles are a good candidate for being the legendary key," the woman concluded.

"What you're suggesting is pretty far out," I responded. "Let me see if I understand you correctly. What you're proposing is that the whistles may be an element in an ancient planetary scheme, concocted by a superior intelligence that had some grand design for us. But who would do such a thing and why?" I asked, perplexed by Yati's grandiose speculation.

By now I was out of breath from the climb. When we began our hike, just outside the village, the trail had followed a small, fast-moving river with large deciduous trees growing along its banks. My duffle packed with whistles had been an easy load then. I had enjoyed the sight of the village women washing their clothes in the river while their children played nearby. The thick foliage formed a canopy overhead. The lush greens and mottled brown shadows on the trail gave me the feeling I was walking in a remote jungle. If it hadn't been for the children's shouts and the sight of the women's laundry spread out on the rocks and bushes, I might have expected a jaguar to slink out of the underbrush. Eventually the trail changed to a narrow path that wound its way up the side of a cliff. My duffle seemed heavy now, and the tropical mid-day sun made the climb uncomfortable.

"Why would anyone create a global treasure hunt?" I asked. "For what possible reason?" I said, reiterating my question as I struggled toward the top.

"To somehow aid in the evolution of human consciousness," Yati answered in earnest. I glanced over at her. With her sturdy walking shoes, the woman looked more like somebody's grandmother from Connecticut than a Dutch metaphysician climbing a cliff toward an ancient Toltec temple.

"If that's the case," I answered, "whoever could conceive and execute such a plan might very well have been able to calculate ahead to the time when our growth had reached a level that would enable us to find the 'key.' At that point in our development we would be capable of both recognizing the key and then transporting it halfway around the world."

"That's almost it," Yati agreed, "except for your use of the word *growth*. Perhaps our present state of separation and alienation is the result of losing our way. The story of man's exclusion from the 'Garden' could be a primal metaphor for forgetting our place in the Creation. Our movement as a species may resemble that of a pendulum; the further we get from our center the greater the energy pulls us to return. Retrieving the arcane knowledge may be a path that will enable us to find our way home again.

"Please don't misunderstand me. I'm not saying you're wasting your time taking the whistles back to Peru. They were probably designed to manifest an increasing potential when played in certain places—ancient ruins, for instance. The whistles have captured your interest because of their psychological effect. They've survived in Peru because of their value in bringing about some kind of psycho-spiritual response. That effect, though, may only be a part of their function. I think the sound is meant to resonate elsewhere. Egypt perhaps," Yati theorized.

"The uniqueness of the sound makes it unlikely that it would also be created in the Middle East or Africa," she continued, following up on her thought. "At the same time, the instruments were perpetuated in an area where an awareness of the spiritual dimension is a paramount aspect of life. If the sounds are the acoustical key, their efficacy in arousing a human response to the spiritual is what has ensured them against being lost through the centuries."

"Supposing you're right," I said. "Who do you think is responsible for constructing this global puzzle?"

"How should I know?" Yati replied, looking directly into my eyes. "Maybe that's why I'm climbing this damn mountain with you."

Several days later, after playing the whistles in various pre-

Columbian monuments, my question remained unanswered. In fact, nothing dramatic had happened at all. The whistles elicited the same response as they had in the States and, indeed, the group was drawn closer together by the sounds. Often, Yati would turn her face toward the sky while blowing into her instrument. Later she remarked that she felt compelled "to play to the sun."

Rosa, a short, stocky woman of Spanish-Indian descent, was increasingly affected by the sounds. As silent as a shadow, this woman of indeterminate age and unknown circumstance accompanied us as we clambered about the ruins. I could see that Rosa was deeply moved whenever we played the whistles. I also noticed that after each meditation she would leave a handful of cornhusks on the ground where we'd been sitting. Our journey together culminated at our last meditation on the December full moon at Teotihuacán.

This sprawling ceremonial center had been built, I conjectured, on a site where something of nearly unimaginable magnitude had once taken place. Nothing less could explain the existence of the Pyramid of the Sun and the Pyramid of the Moon, two immense manmade mountains set in the midst of an otherwise uninterrupted plain. Huge stone steps led to the summit of each edifice, as if constructed for giants who conspired to visit the sky.

Late in the afternoon, having explored the abandoned ceremonial metropolis for hours, our small band ascended to the top of the oldest shrine, the imposing step-pyramid dedicated to the moon. Once again we formed our circle and began to play the whistles for what would be the last time before my departure from Mexico. The unique sound filled the air in its inimitable fashion and drew the attention of a young man selling soft drinks. After glancing at us apprehensively, the vendor deserted his commercial enterprise, leaving us alone to continue our meditation.

Though it was a calm, sunny, windless day, a whirlwind suddenly arose at the base of the pyramid. Dust, picked up by the wind, formed a swirling column that rose into the air hundreds of feet, surpassing even the height of the pyramid. For several seconds the column stood still. Then it rushed against the side of the edifice. A torrent of warm air and grit swept through our circle. The strange column continued out across the Valley of Mexico, leaving momentary puffs of dust each time it touched the ground along the way.

Everyone put down their whistle and joined hands. Tears fell from Rosa's dark brown eyes. Then she began to shake. The woman's tremors traveled like waves through everyone's joined hands. I felt connected to a bioelectric current. Waves of energy surged through my arms and across my chest. Everyone held on. Finally, as if touched in some primeval depth, Rosa began to wail. Within seconds the woman's cry turned into a strange guttural chant. Although her chant lasted only a minute or two, it seemed much longer. Finally, Rosa's voice faded into the silence that surrounded us, and she returned to her normal stoic self. No one said anything. Everyone was listening intently. I listened, too. All I could hear was the residual hum from the whistles ringing in my ears.

As we carefully made our way down the steep stone steps of the pyramid, I asked Yati what Rosa had said in her chant. "I don't know," Yati replied pensively. "Rosa was speaking in a language that none of us has ever heard. Whatever those words mean, they're in the wind now—along with the sounds of your whistles."

The body is the only part of the Earth we feel
from within.

—*Charles Boultenhouse*

THE ASSORTMENT OF PASSENGERS waiting at the airport in Mexico City for the midnight flight to Ecuador looked like a casting call for a movie. I couldn't imagine what all the people were
carrying onto the plane in their blanket rolls and weather-beaten
suitcases. Neither was it likely that any of them could have imagined
the seven pottery whistles safely packed away in the brown canvas
satchel I carried onto the plane. Except for the spontaneous out-
break of wild applause by the passengers when we landed in Quito
the following morning, the flight was uneventful.

My visit to the country on the equator was to rendezvous with
my friends, Andrew Weil, and his companion, Mahina. I had met
Andy in California and had very much enjoyed the company of
this good-natured physician. Andy's book, *The Natural Mind*,[1] had
established his reputation as an articulate explorer of psychotropic
substances and unusual realms of consciousness.

Whenever I had occasion to drive through Arizona I made it
a point to stop at Andy's and Mahina's home in Tucson. My occasional visit was a welcome respite for me. I looked forward to the

hospitality of this genial couple, and I enjoyed an occasional walk into the quiet grandeur of the Saguaro cactus forest that flourished behind their home. Our plan was to meet in Quito and to travel on to Peru together.

I spotted Andy from my taxi, walking with his rambling, bear-like gait toward a session of an international symposium being held to consider a proposed ban on the cultivation of the coca plant. "We're at the Embassy Hotel," Andy shouted to me across the impenetrable lanes of traffic that prevented me from reaching the opposite sidewalk. "We'll meet you there later."

When I finally caught up with Andy and Mahina I learned that two of their friends wished to join our impromptu expedition. At the last minute, Chris and Steve had flown to Quito with the expectation of accompanying us to Peru. Like Andy and Mahina, the men were experienced hikers. Both Chris and Steve had experienced the whistles at Andy's home in Tucson. They were excited by the prospect of playing the replica instruments in Peru. I was happy to have the company of this gregarious group. Now I was assured of being able to play at least five of the whistles along the way.

Steve was a longstanding member of the Rainbow Family and, although I had not met him before, I immediately liked this tall, thin man with his homemade moccasins and lighthearted smile. Steve told me that his friends called him "Smiling Eagle," and that he was famous for his gourmet popcorn. I responded that I hadn't thought to bring popcorn with me, but it seemed a splendid idea.

Our little group spent a few days together in Quito getting acquainted. I viewed my time in the Ecuadorian capital—at an elevation of 10,000 feet—as an opportunity to get used to the higher elevations I would encounter on the Inca Trail in Peru. For several hours each day, I would put on my backpack and hike the city streets. We were tourists together: we hired a taxi and drove out of the city to a spot that had been surveyed as the equator. Later that evening we visited a coffeehouse to listen to local musicians. Early the next morning, the group boarded a plane to Lima; from there we would take another plane to Cuzco.

As we retraced the route I had previously taken to the Inca capital city, I thought about what had transpired in the three years since my initial visit to Peru. Working with Mr. Binkele had enabled me to make and distribute at least a hundred sets of instruments. Gazing out the window of the airplane, I mentally retraced my wanderings with the vessels. Back and forth, I had criss-crossed the country dropping off sets of whistles in Eldridge, Missouri, and Hot Springs, Arkansas; in Oracle, Arizona, and Monticello, Kentucky; in Portsmouth, New Hampshire, and Washington, Massachusetts; in Columbia, Maryland; Ft. Worth, Texas; and Portland, Oregon. I had sent sets to Colorado, Idaho, Hawaii, Vancouver, Toronto, Sweden, Germany, and India. Clusters of them existed in California and New Mexico.

The people who had received vessels were members of ashrams and college professors, free thinkers and oncologists, women's groups and rainbow warriors. I had played the whistles in diverse places: in the Sierra Nevadas and on a Hollywood rooftop; in a Beverly Hills mansion and on the white sands of the desert near Alamogordo, New Mexico; with a Huichol Indian shaman in Big Sur, a medical doctor turned spiritual healer in Apple Valley, and a seeker of Peyote visions in the Jemez Mountains. I had played them with physicists and cancer patients, college students and UFO hunters, pyramidologists and movie stars.

I couldn't remember all of the sets I had delivered. I didn't even know how many I had made. Seven years had passed since my discovery in Pennsylvania of that lone Chimú whistle. In terms of the generations and cultures that had originally produced the vessels, those years were but a brief moment. In an even shorter period of time, a network of hundreds of instruments had been brought into form. Despite the continuance of the academic interpretation that the whistle feature was originally intended as an amusement, many people treasured the sounds from the vessels. Now I was carrying a set of replica instruments back to the land of their origin.

Finally our plane descended, and once again Cuzco appeared beneath the clouds to greet us. My baggage consisted of a backpack containing all my personal gear and the canvas duffle bag that contained the carefully wrapped whistles. I had checked the backpack through along the way, but I had carried the duffle onto each plane. Although the canvas bag was slightly oversized for carry-on luggage, I had convinced a series of airport officials to allow me to carry it on board, explaining that the canvas satchel contained delicate pottery that I was afraid would otherwise break. I had guarded the vessels like a mother hen for most of my journey. In the process I had developed a sense of urgency to get the instruments to Peru.

I was a messenger carrying out a mission ... a mission that had waited centuries for my arrival. I was apprehensive that certain forces—the same forces that had allowed the Spanish to conquer the Indians' civilization and obliterate the native spiritual traditions—might create obstacles in my path. I worried that the forces that had enabled Pizarro's victory were still operable and would thwart the whistles' return. My hope was that if I could "get through" with the replica instruments, they might revive the old spiritual energies—only this time the Indians would prevail.

Anthropologists who worked in remote villages of the Andes had uncovered a myth that gave substance to my fantasy. Once upon a time a mythical being called "Inca-ri," it was believed, founded the city of Cuzco at the spot where a gold rod embedded itself in the earth. Eventually a white chieftain killed Inca-ri, and the dead man's head was buried near Lima. Since then, according to the myth, the head has slowly been growing, and one day it will return, complete with its body.[2]

A local legend in Cuzco added fuel to my imaginings. The legend tells of an Inca prince who had been walled up in a tower of the Catholic cathedral there. According to the story, when the tower falls, the Inca will emerge to claim his birthright and free his people. After the earthquake in May 1950, thousands of Indians gathered in the plaza in front of the church, waiting hopefully for the tower to collapse. Despite severe damage, however, it survived.

Perhaps the myths and legends and the Indians' stolid hope in the aftermath of the earthquake had begun to shake the rigid underpinnings of Spanish domination. Now the whistles might be able to free more of the same spiritual energy that would one day culminate to restore the Indians' cultural and spiritual heritage. All I knew was that it was of the utmost importance for me to play the whistles in Peru.

It was ironic that the set of whistles, which represented a hoped-for end to my quest, had become objects of such strong attachment for me. Eight years earlier I had started out on a spiritual journey by ostensibly abandoning my materialistic desires. Now, it seemed, I had simply replaced one set of compulsions for another.

After checking into the Hotel Viracocha, just a few steps off the main plaza, my companions and I took a taxi to Sacsahuaman. We climbed to the top of the megalithic ruin and formed a circle within the ring of stones where I had surprised myself on my initial visit by washing my hair. For the first time in four centuries, the mysterious sounds of the whistles rang forth from the summit of the oldest shrine in the former Inca capital. Esoteric traditions teach that etheric lines connect the immense wall to every shrine in the old city. I imagined the sounds stirring invisible channels that had lain dormant since the Spanish conquest. The wave might be ten or a hundred years in forming, but the molecules of sacred air had trembled, and the etheric realm had moved.

For three years I had worked at molding a clay shell around an empty space. I had lectured to thousands of people that playing the vessels was a means to become empty and receptive—like the vessel itself. I had taught that entering into stillness was where meditation begins. Somewhere between Santa Fe and Cuzco I had forgotten what I had so often preached. As I played the whistles now, at Sacsahuaman, my mind raced with the idea that the legends of the headless Inca and the Inca entombed in the tower were metaphors for the Indian's spiritual heritage that had been severed from the Indian's body. I imagined that the return of the whistles to Cuzco would somehow heal the dismemberment. The end of the old story was in sight, the legend would be fulfilled, and the Indian would be returned to wholeness.

Descending to the grassy plain in front of the megalithic ruin, we reformed our circle and once again began to play the replica vessels. Within a few minutes, the caretaker of the monument, a middle-aged Indian wearing Western clothes and a yellow plastic construction helmet to shade his face from the high-altitude sun, walked over to where we were sitting. Beneath the helmet, the caretaker's face was a classic Indian profile from the old empire. I motioned the man toward an empty spot in our circle and stood up to hand him a whistle. We both sat down, and everyone began to play.

The swirl of our mantra reverberated against the enigmatic wall. For me, time wavered backward and forward. I saw and heard a visual and sonic tapestry: European and Indian, sound and stone that combined to fulfill the scenario I had long envisioned. When the sounds stopped, the Indian who had joined us replaced his whistle on the grass. Nodding his head, he walked away. As the man turned toward me again, I noticed a faded word that someone had written with a marking pen on the visor of his construction helmet. Although the black ink had faded into the yellow plastic, I could still trace the letters. "Inca," it said. I had played my whistles with a descendent of the Incas.

The Cuzco market had not changed in the three years since my first visit. My companions and I separated, each with an assignment to buy provisions for the hike. Unlike before, I purchased my coca directly from the Indians. Andy guided me to a section of the market that apparently had been closed during my earlier visit, a temporary victim of the vacillating governmental policy regarding the sale of the sacred plant. Now, however, a row of Indian women sat on the ground behind great mounds of coca leaves set out on blankets in front of them. Each had a supply of plastic bags and a balance scale as well as various sized lumps of tokra for sale. Following my friend's example, I sampled leaves from each woman's pile. Some were dry and brittle and others were soft and pliable; some smelled musty and still others tasted bitter.

"How do you choose which ones to buy?" I finally asked.

"I think it's a matter of personal taste," Andy replied. "The Indians prefer the mild, aromatic leaf over the bitter leaf. The bitter leaf contains the highest percentage of the cocaine alkaloid. Another thirteen pharmacologically active compounds are in the leaf as well. It's unfortunate that only the so-called active principle, cocaine, has received all of the attention. The other substances working in combination with each other have an entirely different effect, very likely providing a kind of pharmacological insulation that ensures against the misuse of the isolated cocaine alkaloid.

"The problem with refining natural substances into white powders is that the process strips away the elements that serve to dictate their appropriate use. Isolated and refined drugs are much more toxic than their botanical sources. The concentrated form tends to increase the likelihood for abuse." Andy paused to show me how to pull the stem out of each leaf so I could prevent the sharp ends of the tiny sticks from scratching the inside of my cheek. I hadn't known to remove them on my first visit, and I could still remember the soreness that had stayed with me for several weeks after my return to the States.

"In the late nineteenth century the occasional abuse of cocaine was sensationalized by the press," Andy continued. "A fear was promulgated that coca was the same as opium in its harmful effect on physical and mental health. In just a few years, coca went from being praised as the most beneficial stimulant tonic known to man to being vigorously condemned as a dangerous narcotic. The result was a legal ban that halted experimentation with the leaves. Only a few specialized uses of cocaine, such as in anesthesia, were regarded as acceptable.

"In highland communities, coca is considered a 'force sustaining food,'" Andy added. "Researchers have reported that the combination of alkaloids enables the hemoglobin in our blood to absorb up to 30 percent more oxygen. That factor is especially important for people like us who are used to living and working at lower altitudes. While hiking we will be carrying our backpacks for hours at altitudes well above ten thousand feet. Without the coca to enable a higher input of oxygen, the hike would certainly be a struggle for some of us."

Later that afternoon the five of us boarded the train to Machu Picchu. We traveled for several hours and then the train stopped briefly at Kilometer-88, the drop-off point for hikers of the Inca Trail, and left us standing beside the tracks in an uninhabited stretch of the Urubamba Valley gorge. Along with my provisions, I carried three of the whistles in my backpack, having prevailed upon each of my companions to carry one instrument as well.

Our first challenge came within fifty yards of the railroad tracks. A few steps led diagonally down the embankment to a stone buttress where a pair of steel cables spanned the narrow gorge perhaps forty feet above the raging river. Suspended from one cable by two antique cast-iron pulleys, a rickety wooden platform swayed precariously over the gorge. The second cable provided a means to pull the swinging perch from one side of the riverbank to the other. For a small fee, an enterprising Indian ferryman piloted the questionable conveyance.

"I can see why the Incas held a special ceremony for crossing rivers," I exclaimed, half-jokingly. The reason for the river-crossing ceremony, I had learned, was to acknowledge the spirit of the river, as well as to cause each traveler to pause, and therefore search out the best route, before attempting a crossing.

"It's the only way across," Mahina lamented, looking down into the river. All of us could hear the ominous sound of rocks grinding against each other from the surging force of the rushing water.

The platform was capable of carrying two passengers at a time plus a mound of backpacks. I scrambled up to the front of the hanging swing and sat with my legs dangling over the edge. With one hand I grasped a suspension cable and with the other I held onto one of the backpacks in the center of the platform. I didn't notice that the second cable, the one used to pull the platform across the gorge, passed very close to the side of my head. It's a short trip, I thought to myself, less than half a minute. Maybe if I close my eyes, when I open them again I'll be on the other side. At the last moment I decided to leave them open.

With a sudden lurch and no forewarning, the Indian launched the precarious contrivance. Almost smoothly, the platform swung out over the gorge, its weight causing us to drop ten or twelve feet toward the tumultuous river. Reaching the end of its momentum, the platform suddenly snapped back to within inches of the second cable.

Glancing up, I glimpsed the second cable hurtling toward my head from above. Instinctively, I rolled over, narrowly averting a catastrophe. The cable continued on its life-threatening trajectory, passing through the space where my head had been only seconds before. The tremendous rush of adrenaline that coursed through my body washed away my self-centered preoccupation with completing my mission and jolted my awareness into the present moment. Like the old Inca ritual, crossing the river had served to focus my attention on the immediacy of the world around me.

The pottery whistles had made it this far. If they were meant to survive the hike and be played in some unforeseen place, that would happen despite my myopic concern. The only way I could help to fulfill the destiny of the instruments was to be as conscious as possible.

"The next time we cross this river, it will be by bridge at Machu Picchu," I remarked, as we regrouped on the other side of the gorge. It was already late in the afternoon, so, following the trail for several hundred yards up-river, we pitched camp for the night in a grove of eucalyptus trees.

We started a fire with some twigs and put a pot of vegetables on to boil. Along with fresh carrots, potatoes, and leeks, Mahina had found some giant cloves of garlic and hot, spicy chili pepper in the market. Within a half-hour each of us had a warm bowl in our hands that contained the vegetables along with a savory broth that we sopped up with chunks of brown bread. Chris had purchased some marinated black olives that tasted like the Greek Kalamatas. A hard, grainy chocolate rounded out our meal.

After supper we relaxed around the little fire. Sipping from steaming mugs of mint tea, we talked about the legendary trail we were about to hike. "According to this map," Andy commented, looking in a guidebook he had found in Cuzco, "we won't really pick up what looks like an Inca road for a couple of days— although ruins are scattered all along the way. What we'll be following at first are mainly mountain paths used by shepherds."

"I suspect that more ruins will be discovered in years to come," I added. "I don't think any of them will be overrun by hordes of tourists, though. Not unless the government strings a cable car over these mountains. After all, the Inca Trail was rediscovered in 1915, but it wasn't until recently that it was explored in any detail. The terrain is arduous."

"I'm surprised the Inca Trail wasn't discovered before then," Steve remarked. "Hundreds of years have passed since the conquest, and the Spanish really scoured these mountains looking for treasure. The colonial garrison searched for the rebel Inca and his forces for many years as well. They might have found the trail then."

"Did you notice the terrain for the last twenty miles or so of the train ride?" I asked him. "Sections of it are impassable, sheer cliffs enshrouded in a tangle of jungle that plunge to the river. Only the construction of causeways in the twentieth century made it possible to bring the railroad through. The over-the-mountain approach is very difficult as well. Portions of the Inca roads can't accommodate a horse and rider, either, only a man on foot.

"I've heard a legend that Machu Picchu was a sacred city," I added. "Supposedly, the city was protected in some magical way from the Spaniards who would have torn it down in their campaign to wipe out Indian superstition and religion."

"It's hard to imagine all they destroyed," Mahina reflected. "The only thing the conquistadors seemed interested in was the Indians' gold and silver; nothing else was important to them."

"Maybe that's why the whistles survived," I remarked. "If the Spaniards had suspected that the pottery vessels were spiritual implements or, for that matter, had anything to do with Indian spirituality, they would have branded them 'instruments of the devil' and smashed them with the other shrines they destroyed. It may turn out that what they stole wasn't the real treasure at all."

"Let's get some sleep," Mahina suggested. "From the looks of these mountains we're going to need all our energy tomorrow."

Not only did we need all our energy the next day, but for days afterward. From the very beginning the hike was arduous. The entire second and third day we spent in what seemed to be a relentless and interminable ascent from the Urubamba River to the summit of "Dead Woman's Pass," 13,770 feet above sea level. It was a grueling climb, punctuated by frequent coca stops. The trail, however, was well marked. Sometimes it cut through thick vegetation and at other times meandered across open stretches of mountainside. Water was abundant. The mountains were alive with springs that gushed from the hillsides or ran in narrow rivulets toward the Urubamba River far below. To avoid contamination from animals pasturing at the higher elevations, we drank and filled our water bottles from springs as they came out of the hills. The coca was essential. Without the leaves, the forty-pound load on my back would have been unbearable.

We passed a few villages along the way—small settlements composed of primitive huts. The only people to be seen, however, were an occasional shepherd and a few children. One little girl shyly approached us as we rested next to a stream. Her dress was made entirely of patches roughly sewn together. The child smiled at us from her dirt-smeared face that spoke to our entire torn century.

"The foreign-aid programs never really reach these people," Chris remarked, expressing a helplessness we all felt.

Steve gave the girl a piece of an apple he was eating. Before devouring it, she carefully removed and tucked away the seeds, as if they were some rare and valuable treasure. The altitude, of course, was too high for apple trees to grow.

Late in the afternoon of the third day we crossed our second major pass, the Abra de Runkuracay at 13,120 feet. We climbed a precipitous flight of stone steps to an ancient settlement built on a mountain shelf. With a sigh of relief, I shed the burden of my pack and collapsed on the ground. I was exhausted to the point of being too tired to eat. After removing my boots, which had been thoroughly soaked by intermittent afternoon rains, I fell into a deep sleep against an Inca wall.

When I awoke in the morning I could see, in the valley beneath the high bluff on which we had camped, a narrow ribbon of white granite blocks that climbed across the flank of the mountain toward the third and final pass. We had reached the Inca Trail. From this point on, I supposed, the trail would descend and the hike would be less strenuous. I was half-right. The path did descend after we had crossed the last pass at just over 12,000 feet, but the descent was an exceedingly steep, bone-jarring ordeal.

Our mid-afternoon climb down what amounted to a thousand-foot, near-vertical cliff covered by heavy jungle growth was a nightmare. Even with vines and creepers to hold onto, the trail would have been barely negotiable under ideal conditions. As luck would have it, we had rain. The water quickly turned the yard-wide dirt track into a mudslide that zigzagged through the thick under-brush. For much of the way the vegetation completely encircled the trail, giving the path the manageability of a mud-slick burrow.

It was impossible for me to remain on my feet for more than a few steps at a time. My descent was really a series of controlled falls from one switchback to the next. For most of the way I thought we were lost. This couldn't possibly be "The Inca Trail." I decided that the safest way down was to slide on my heels. The bottom of my backpack and my rear end served as "outriggers," both to sta-bilize and allow me the freedom to slow myself down by catching hold of the underbrush along the way. As I watched my companions make a similar descent, I momentarily wondered if the pottery whistles would survive intact.

"This is the reason Machu Picchu wasn't discovered by the Spaniards," Mahina declared during a pause in our clumsy descent. "A horse couldn't get through this brush, and it certainly doesn't look like anyone would build a settlement down here either."

Mahina was probably correct. Until the twentieth century there hadn't been an approach to Machu Picchu from the river, and the Inca city wasn't visible from the bottom of the gorge. Unless the trail had been intentionally disguised, undoubtedly one or another of the Spanish scouts had found the beautiful hewn granite path that we had followed over the last pass. Anyone looking down into the gorge from above, however, would conclude that the mountainside was inhospitable. Building a substantial settlement on the side of that mountain would have been unimaginable.

At last we burst out of the underbrush onto a definite trail that traversed the mountainside. Several Indian workmen who were clearing the trail stared at us in astonishment, confirming my suspicion that we had just taken an unusual route for our descent.

"Which way to Machu Picchu?" Andy asked one of the men.

The man pointed to the trail on the other side of a wide swath of rocks that were blocking the pathway.

"Wouldn't you know it," Mahina sighed.

Holding our breaths, we inched our way for about twenty yards over the loose, wet shale until once again we were on solid ground. Now, however, the path turned into a narrow ledge that traced the mountain wall high above the Urubamba Valley. In places the rain-slick walkway was only a few feet wide. A misstep on the well-worn rocks would mean a plunge into the abyss. The trail widened, cutting through a forest comprised of giant ferns, twenty feet tall. The fern forest was shady and moist. Water dripped from the huge leaves, and I wondered what sort of creatures made their home there. My boot bumped against a stone outcropping, and a dozen pitch-black, velvety moths flew out of a crevice, fluttering—as if blinded by the daylight—around my ankles.

Finally, we turned a corner and there in front of us, nestled on a jagged mountain spur, was a tiny stone town exquisitely perched amidst the emerald green jungle. We had arrived at Huinay-Huayna.[3] The little town was stunning, an architectural master-piece set two thousand feet above the river, with a breathtaking view of the Urubamba Valley gorge and the snow-capped ramparts of Mt. Veronica.

A long flight of stone steps connected the upper and lower sec-tions of the settlement. On one side of the stairway, agricultural terraces traced the contours of the steep mountainside. On the other side of the stairway, a series of ten cascade pools, constructed from granite blocks, directed the flow of water from a stream that trickled out of the mountain. At the base of the staircase, perfectly preserved, stood a miniature town complete with its own tiny square. Surmounting the site, another cluster of buildings flanked a semi-circular tower with seven trapezoidal windows, each of which framed its own picture of the stupendous view.

"You could grow enough food on these terraces to feed a city," Steve exclaimed as we shed our packs.

"Or supply a constant stream of pilgrims on their way to Machu Picchu," I added, splashing water from one of the cascade pools over my head.

My companions and I drifted apart, each of us absorbed by the exquisite little village that time had preserved on its nearly inac-cessible mountain. I descended the long staircase to the lower sec-tion of the town and found, on the other side of a low retaining wall, a small stone platform that jutted out over a breathtaking plunge to the bottom of the gorge.

I scaled the wall and sat on the shelf. There I was, perched on a ledge in the sky. Clouds were floating by at eye level. I could see, far away at the bottom of the gorge, the train from Cuzco winding its way toward Machu Picchu. I remembered my excitement as a passenger when I had ridden that train for the first time. Like me, the people on the train had been moved to make a journey, to experience for themselves the aura of the legendary Inca city. Although many of them had come here as tourists, all were on a pilgrimage of some sort.

From my vantage point the train looked tiny. I envisioned the passengers looking out the windows at the churning river, preparing to disembark. If they could see me at all, sitting on this ledge, I would appear as a tiny speck too. Tomorrow, when I reached Machu Picchu, I would meet some of the people from that train — people like me, whose path had brought them here now.

I wondered, Were we all really bits of sentient clay, sparked with life and breath? Had we forgotten, in the search for our spirit, that our roots were in the Earth? The people who had built here, whose shrines still beckoned us, knew the profundity of both aspects of our being. We are vessels crafted from clay, enlivened by the breath of our Creator. And so these people named us well: *Alpacamasca,* Animated Earth.

Epilogue

IF YOU FEEL I'VE LEFT YOU HANGING, you're not alone. Since *Animated Earth* was first published in 1987, a number of people have asked, "Please tell me, what happened next?" or, "Did you play the whistles at Machu Picchu?" or, "How does the story end?" Occasionally I have been able to answer one of these questions or recount a pertinent anecdote. No finite ending to *Animated Earth* exists, although other possibilities for ending the story have occurred to me.

For instance, I might have ended this book in the year following my second trip to Machu Picchu, when I moved to Florida to become a writer. I didn't take the whistles with me to Florida. I didn't even tell anyone there about my journey with the old instruments. At the time, I needed to find my identity outside of the magnificent obsession that for so many years had animated *my* life. As I began to write, however, I thought about telling the story of my journey. Thus this book was born and the whistles were present once again in my life.

I might have ended the story of *Animated Earth* a few years later, when I received an invitation to bring the whistles to Hopi Land to play with a group of elders. I accepted the invitation and went to Arizona with the set of original vessels I had assembled. That journey to the Hopi's ancestral home resulted in my making a promise to two of the elders to craft for them two sets of instruments. As it turned out, both elders were subsequently invited to the United Nations to tell their people's prophecy to the General Assembly. I wondered if the sounds from the old whistles had in some measure furthered their journey, as they had my own.

This book had other possible endings. For instance, I might have told the story of how I taught two apprentices the craft of whistle making and then watched as they made sets of whistles for hundreds of others who wished to explore the sound energy for themselves. Or I might have ended the story at a workshop for sound healers, or tracked the number of such people and groups who have chosen to use the whistles for healing. Dr. Donnan's speculation that, if left unchecked, I might suggest the whistles had originally been used for healing had come true.

One or another surprise endings might have provided a sort of Möbius strip finale to the story. For example, twenty years after getting kicked out of UCLA, I found myself playing a set of my whistles with the publisher of the *Los Angeles Times*. The provocative headline for George Alexander's article had catapulted me out of my idyllic life at UCLA and had given me the impetus to travel to Peru. While on that journey I had been inspired to replicate the vessels. Now I was playing a set of those whistles with the man whose newspaper had helped to initiate that branching, and so the story turned back on itself.

I might have ended *Animated Earth* with an account of watching a video of an indigenous Mayan shaman performing a ceremony in Guatemala. In a somber cave illuminated by hundreds of candles, the man chanted numbers from his people's sacred calendar. After the shaman's rhythmic count was completed, I watched the man and his companions put a set of whistles to their lips to sound forth the unique effect I had rediscovered in that New York hotel room. As I watched the video clip and listened to the recorded sounds from my whistles reverberate within the cave, I remembered the solstice radio broadcast where my aspirations had been dashed. The world didn't need me to become a modern interpreter of ancient Mayan calendrics. Authentic interpreters of that cosmology had survived.

These examples are mostly outer endings, though, elements of a narrative that trace multiple journeys the whistles have taken, with me in tow. A number of other possibilities for ending this story relate to my inner exploration. In this vein, I might have ended *Animated Earth* in 1983, when I was writing a short story about the siege at Sacsahuaman. To my surprise, I discovered that a few lines of the story's dialogue had taken shape as a poem. I've included that poem at the beginning of chapter 9 in this edition of *Animated Earth.* Writing those brief but poignant lines was another beginning that enabled me to discover the heart of a poet within myself.

I might have ended this second edition of *Animated Earth* with the story of a gifted sound healer whom I met in 2002 at a sound-healing workshop in Loveland, Colorado. After this woman toned into my chest, I felt the last vestige of my fear of abandonment release from my heart. Later that night I had a dream. In the dream I saw two wraiths pass close by. I felt as if they might have emerged from my own left shoulder. Within moments the apparitions disappeared into the night. The wraiths were my twin fears: my fear of abandonment and my fear of commitment. Both fears had been impervious to all manner of therapy. In the morning I awoke, knowing I finally had been released from what had been an intractable bondage. Ciana, too, had been correct. Something within my consciousness had finally changed.

I might have ended this book when I married Mara in 1984. My whistle apprentice, Don Wright, introduced us. Our marriage resulted in the births of our two sons, Jacob and Isaac. As I watched each baby come into this world, my heart opened to a love I might otherwise have never known. Even though our family has known sorrow, I continue to experience the immeasurable love a father can feel for his children. Once again, my journey with the whistles had opened a pathway to my heart.

Finally, I might have ended *Animated Earth* with a reflection about a small boy playing with his stick in a muddy, water-filled hole. Some unknown force enabled that child to escape from the hole and allowed him to breathe without having to stand on the tips of his toes. I still wonder how that frightened, mud-smeared child grew up to be a man who now sits with another stick in his hand, stirring and prodding his clay.

And yet my mind even now returns to that little ledge in the sky on the way to Machu Picchu. What I imagined then, as I watched the passenger train approaching from Cuzco, has happened and will continue to happen. Tomorrow or the next day or the day after, I will meet another pilgrim on this path, and the story will begin anew.

Notes

Chapter 2

1. Sat Prem, *Sri Aurobindo or the Adventure of Consciousness* (Delhi: The Mother's Institute of Consciousness, 1970), 213ff.

Chapter 3

1. In 1602 a mining company was formed to divert the Moche River against the enormous pyramid. Before its partial destruction as a result of this dubious enterprise, the base of the pyramid was a terrace 750 feet long, 450 feet wide, and 60 feet high. Upon this base stood another pyramid 340 feet square and 75 feet high.

2. In 1984, I legally changed my name back to its original Russian form, Statnekov. Before then I had used the shorter "Stat."

Chapter 4

1. P. J. Arriaga, *The Extirpation of Idolatry in Peru* (Lima, 1621).

2. Father B. Cobo, *History of the New World* (Seville, 1890–1895).

Chapter 5

1. See Guido F. Smoorenburg, "Combination Tones and Their Origin," *Journal of the Acoustical Society of America*, Vol. 52, No. 2 (1972).

2. Houston Smith, et al., "On an Unusual Mode of Chanting by Certain Tibetan Lamas," *Journal of the Acoustical Society of America*, Vol. 40, No. 5 (1967).

3. Steven Garrett and Daniel K. Stat, "Peruvian Whistling Bottles," *Journal of the Acoustical Society of America*, Vol. 62, No. 2 (1977).

Chapter 6

1. Stanislav Grof, M.D., *Realms of the Human Unconscious: Observations from LSD Research* (New York: Viking, 1975).

Chapter 7

1. *Los Angeles Times*, Monday, December 13, 1976, Part I, 3.

Chapter 8

1. W. Golden Mortimer, M.D., *History of Coca, The Divine Plant of the Incas* (New York, 1901: reprint San Francisco: AND/OR Press, 1974), 205.

2. Mariano Rivero and J. J. Von Tschudi, *Peruvian Antiquities* (New York, 1854; reprint New York: Kraus Reprint Co., 1971), 85.

3. Ibid., 87.

4. Alfred Metraux, *The History of the Incas* (New York: Schocken Books, 1970), 51.

Chapter 12

1. "The Great Invocation," Distributed by the Lucis Trust, Suite 566, 866 United Nations Plaza, New York, NY 10017-1888.

Chapter 15

1. John Michell, *The View Over Atlantis* (New York: Ballantine Books, 1969).

Chapter 16

1. Andrew Weil, *The Natural Mind: A New Way of Looking at Drugs and the Higher Consciousness* (Boston: Houghton Mifflin Co., 1972).

2. Alfred Metraux, *The History of the Incas* (New York: Schocken Books, 1970), 196.

3. Pronounced *Win-ee, Why-nuh;* the name of a little flower that grows in the area. In English it means "forever young."